Breed Standard for the West Highland White Terrier

BODY

Compact. Back level, loins broad and strong. Chest deep and ribs well arched in upper half presenting a flattish side appearance. Back ribs of considerable depth and distance from last rib of quarters as short as compatible with free movement of body.

TAIL

12.5–15 cms (5–6 ins) long, covered with harsh hair, no feathering, as straight as possible, carried jauntily, not gay or carried over back.

HINDQUARTERS

Strong, muscular and wide across top. Legs short, muscular sinewy. Thighs very muscular and not too wide apart. Hocks bent and well set in under body so as to be fairly close to each other when standing or moving.

COAT

Double coated. Outer coat consists of harsh hair, about 5 cms (2 ins) long, free from any curl. Undercoat, which resembles fur, short, soft and close.

COLOUR

White.

SIZE

Height at withers approximately 28 cms (11 ins).

FEET

Forefeet larger than hind, round, proportionate in size, strong, thickly padded and covered with short harsh hair. Hindfeet are smaller and thickly padded. Under surface of pads and all nails preferably black.

West Highland White Terrier

by Penelope Ruggles-Smythe

Table of Contents

DISTRIBUTED BY:
INTERPET
P U B L I S H I N G
Vincent Lane, Dorking
Surrey RH4 3YX England

ISBN 13: 978 1 902389 12 7

81

Housebreaking and Training Your West Highland White Terrier

by Charlotte Schwartz

Be informed about the importance of training your Westie, from the basics of housebreaking, and understanding the development of a young dog, to executing obedience commands (sit, stay, down, etc.).

Photographers:
Isabelle Francais, Carol Ann Johnson and Antonio Philippe

Additional photos by:

Norvia Behling
Carolina Biological Supply
Liza Clancy
Kent and Donna Dannen
Doskocil
James Hayden-Yoav
James R. Hayden, RBP
Dwight R. Kuhn
Dr Dennis Kunkel
Nancy Liguori
Alice Pantfoeder
Mikki Pet Products
Phototake

Jean Claude Revy
Dr Andrew Spielman
Nikki Sussman
Karen Taylor
Alice van Kempen
C. James Webb
Illustrations by: Renée Low
The Publisher wishes to thank:
Vera Agnello
Doug and Joan Calhoun
Philippe Coppe
Natalie Cuccioli
Maryse Delaye

106

Health Care of Your West Highland White Terrier

Know how to select a proper veterinary surgeon and care for your dog at all stages of life. Topics include vaccination scheduling, skin problems, dealing with external and internal parasites and the medical conditions common to the breed.

131

Your Senior West Highland White Terrier

Recognise the signs of an ageing dog, both behavioural and medical; implement a senior-care programme with your veterinary surgeon and become comfortable with making the final decisions and arrangements for your senior Westie.

141

Understanding the Behaviour of Your West Highland White Terrier

Learn to recognise and handle common behavioural problems in your Westie, including aggression with people and other dogs, chewing, barking, mounting, digging, jumping up, etc.

The forebears of our West Highland White Terriers, from Scotland, were originally solid white-coloured Cairn Terriers. Today's breed possesses a look and character all its own.

ANCESTRY OF THE
West Highland White Terrier

MEET THE WEST HIGHLAND WHITE TERRIER

The West Highland White Terrier! His name says much. A terrier, therefore a breed of earth dog. White! A white dog, neither black, brown nor brindle. And he hails from the West Highlands, surely the little fellow is from Scotland, where the countryside is rugged, the brogues thick, and the dogs courageous.

This book will give you the history, characteristics, and description of the Westie. You will also learn about puppy care, training and the health of the breed. In the colour photographs, you will see that the Westie is cute as a button and a wonderful companion. This may not be the dog for everyone as terriers are active, busy dogs and this breed has a white coat to keep up. However, if you like a plucky, lively dog, one that will be a devoted family member, this may be the dog for you. And, as is true with most other breeds, once you give your heart and home to a Westie, you will remain a devotee to the breed for a lifetime.

An early representative of the West Highland White Terrier, Ch Placemore Prosperity, owned by Mrs Allow.

HISTORY OF THE WHITE TERRIER

In the history of dogs, the West Highland White Terrier is not an ancient breed; however, its official

DID YOU KNOW?

Since dogs have been inbred for centuries, their physical and mental characteristics are constantly being changed to suit man's desires for hunting, retrieving, scenting, guarding, and warming their master's laps. During the past 150 years, dogs have been judged according to physical characteristics as well as functional abilities. Few breeds can boast a genuine balance between physique, working ability and temperament.

terriers fell roughly into two basic categories: the rough-coated, short-legged dogs of Scotland and the longer legged, smooth-coated dogs of England.

The family of Scotch Terriers—those bred in Scotland—divide themselves into the modern Scottish Terrier, the West Highland White Terrier, the Cairn Terrier and the Skye Terrier. In the early 1800s, dogs referred to as the Scotch Terrier could be any of the first three breeds mentioned. Interbreeding was common amongst these breeds and all

Three typical representatives of early Westies from the original Scottish stock: Col. Malcolm's Boidheach, the Countess of Aberdeen's Ch Cromar Snowflake, and Col. Malcolm's Doichioll II.

beginnings, which trace back to the late 1800s, places it amongst one of the older breeds recognised by The Kennel Club.

The West Highland White Terrier belongs to the group of dogs known as terriers, from the Latin word *terra*, meaning *earth*. The terrier is a dog that has been bred to work beneath the ground to drive out small and large vermin, rodents, and other animals that can be a nuisance to country living.

All of the dogs in the Terrier Group originated in the British Isles with the exception of the Miniature Schnauzer, which derives from Germany. Many of the terrier breeds were derived from a similar ancestor and, as recently as the mid-1800s, the

three breed types could come from the same litter.

As breeders started exhibiting at dog shows, it was realised that there must be more uniformity within the breed, i.e., all pups in a litter should look alike as well as being of the same type as their sire and dam.

The Westie's history is better known than the background of some of the other terriers, where the history is often a bit murky and convoluted. In the early 1800s, the Malcolm family of Poltalloch in Argyllshire kept a group of small white dogs. As with all terrier breeders, these dogs were bred for working and not for the show ring. 'Unless they were fit and game for the purpose, their heads were not kept long out of the huge butt of water in the stable yard.' Those who bred and kept dogs had a specific purpose of work for their particular dog—long legs for

At the turn of the 20th century, Ch Brean Glunyiema, owned by Mrs Innes, was considered an ideal Westie of the day.

speed, short legs for going to ground; double coats for protection against the elements, etc.

It is written that the Malcolm clan preferred the white terrier due to a hunting accident in which their favourite sandy-coloured dog was mistaken for a fox and shot. After that, only cream or white terriers were kept for breeding. Whilst some breeders of terriers destroyed their white puppies as they felt that they were not as hardy as the coloured dogs, the Malcolms felt that the white dogs were as courageous and feisty as the coloured ones and proved that the white dog was as able a terrier as any other.

In the mid-1800s there were other strains of white terriers in the Highlands. The Roseneath, bred by gamekeeper George Duke, who was on the staff of the Argyll estates, is in the background of the Cairn Terrier. The Pittenweem Terrier, which was regarded as the

DID YOU KNOW?

Prestigious wins by the West Highland White Terrier: Ch Wolvey Pattern of Edgerstoune, owned by Marion Eppley, was Best in Show at Westminster Kennel Club in New York City in 1942. Barbara Worcester Keenan's Ch Elfinbrook Simon was Best in Show at Westminster in 1962. Ch Ardenrun Andsome of Purston, owned by Dr Alvaro Hunt, was Best in Show at the Montgomery County Kennel Club's all terrier show in the U.S. in 1976. Mrs K Newstead's Ch Dianthus Buttons won Best in Show at Crufts in England in 1976. Derek and Joan Tattersall's Ch Olac Moonpilot was Best in Show at Crufts in 1990.

The term Scotch Terrier could refer to any of the terriers of Scotland, the family of dogs to which the Scottish Terrier belongs.

varminty look about them. They are very active, with a linty-white type of coat, and well-knit together. The coat is hard and bristly, from an inch to two and a half inches in length except on the head and muzzle where it is short, hard and wiry...The head is long, nose broad, the teeth extremely large for so small a dog. The ears are pricked and covered in a short velvety coat. The tail is well-set, slightly curved and carried gaily...I have had the breed and know what they are fit for and may add that no water was ever too cold and no earth ever too deep for them.' The same description fits the dog quite well today.

In the early dog shows, terriers were often shown under the classification of Scotch Terriers and often there would be quite a variety of types in this class. In 1904 the Scottish Kennel Club held the first class for the West

White Scottish Terrier, was a strain that died out fairly early. Sir Malcolm did not care for either the Roseneaths or the Pittenweems and refused to allow any of his dogs to be crossed with these strains. The Poltalloch dogs of the Malcolms were the white strain that moved forward, bred true, and became the foundation of the modern breed. Colonel Sir Ian Malcolms, with his white Poltalloch Terriers, is considered to be the father of the breed, in addition to having given the breed its official name, the West Highland White Terrier.

An early description of these terriers was written by a Captain Mackie and published in *Gray's Dogs of Scotland* in 1891: 'The Poltalloch Whites weighs from 16—20 lb. with a determined

Designed to pursue badgers and otters, the Sealyham Terrier was created in the mid-1900s. The West Highland White Terrier is believed to have been used in the creation of the Sealyham Terrier.

The Cairn Terrier differs from today's West Highland White Terrier in colour and structure, to an extent. The original Westies were merely white Cairns!

Highland White Terrier and in the same year the West Highland White Terrier Club of Scotland was founded with the Duke of Argyll serving as the first president.

In 1907 the first champion of the breed was made up and 141 Westies were registered in Scotland. In the same year Crufts held classes for the breed and the West Highland White Terrier Club of England was formed. The breed grew rapidly after this and prior to World War I, 3947 Westies had been registered and 27 became champions of record.

Some early prominent names in the breed were Holland Buckley and his daughter of the Scotia Kennels, Mrs B Lucas of the Highclere Kennels and Mrs Cyril (May) Pacey of the Wolvey Kennels. The Wolvey Kennels became very well known and eventually produced an impressive 58 champions. By 1916 all dog shows ceased in the British Isles with the onset of World War I. Breeding was greatly curtailed because of the difficulty in finding food due to the strict food-

Col. Malcolm's dogs Sonny and Sarah were typical of the Westie during the early days of their development.

rationing laws. Many breeders had to put down dogs and Mrs Pacey herself had to destroy 15 dogs.

DID YOU KNOW?

Dogs and wolves are members of the genus *Canis*. Wolves are known scientifically as *Canis lupus* while dogs are known as *Canis domesticus*. Dogs and wolves are known to interbreed. The term canine derives from the Latin derived word *Canis*. The term dog has no scientific basis but has been used for thousands of years. The origin of the word dog has never been authoritatively ascertained.

Most breeders tried to retain a few dogs in order to keep going and breeding was allowed again in 1919. By 1920, dog shows resumed and five champions were made up that year.

Mrs Pacey continued her excellent breeding programme and at the time of her death in 1963, 25% of all recorded champions carried the Wolvey prefix. She was well known as a breeder and many of her dogs found their way to the Continent as well as to the Scandinavian countries.

Many outstanding dogs were bred between 1920 and 1940 in England and it was also during this period that professional handlers started showing Westies.

The handlers, with their expertise with the stripping knife, started smartening up the little dog. Owner-handlers followed suit with their grooming in order to keep up with the competition and the Westie eventually took on a 'smart' look rather than the prior 'working' look that the dog had carried in its earlier years.

CROSSING THE ATLANTIC
WESTIES IN THE UNITED STATES
In the early 1900s the white dogs that had been brought to the United States were registered as Roseneath Terriers and in 1906, five were entered at the Westminster Kennel Club dog show under that classification.

Virginia Murray is generally credited with bringing the first West Highland White Terrier to the United States in 1907, and she became a dominant force in the breed for many years. In 1909 the breed was recognised by the American Kennel Club, and the West Highland White Terrier Club of America was admitted to AKC membership in September of that year.

The United States has always had a very dedicated group of Westie fanciers who not only have bred a number of fine Westies but also have imported top dogs from England who have won top honours at

> **DID YOU KNOW?**
> Contrary to what many believe, ('Is that a White or a Black Scottie?') the two dogs on the Scotch bottle are the Scottish Terrier and the West Highland White Terrier. The Scottie has a long muzzle with longer ears placed high on his head; the Westie has a short, broad muzzle with smaller ears. The Scottish Terrier is a much heavier boned and heavier bodied dog than is the Westie.

the shows. More importantly, these English imports have produced American offspring who have continued to do well in the ring and for breeding programmes.

In the late 1920s, Edgerstoune Kennels, owned by Mrs John Winant (later Mrs Marion Eppley), thrived until the 1950s, producing over 40 champions.

The famous drawing by Sir Edwin Landseer (1839) showing a West Highland White Terrier along with other sporting dogs.

In the 1920s a famous German breeder, Mrs Binzwanger, brought the West Highland White Terrier to southern Germany (Bavaria) where they were successful in ratting. She showed her dogs regularly at German dog shows.

Mrs Eppley imported many fine dogs from England, including the great Ch Wolvey Pattern of Edgerstoune. John Marvin noted in his book *The Complete West Highland White Terrier* that Mrs Eppley had 'an astute ability to pick a winner at home or abroad. Some years ago, she judged a show in England and placed a Westie bitch Best in Show. Immediately after the judging, she bought the bitch and brought her back to America. The acquisition was Ch Wolvey Pattern of Edgerstoune, who went Best in Show at Westminster (1942).

Years later, the same situation was repeated. Again in England, Mrs Eppley placed a Scottish Terrier Best in Show and then bought the dog. Ch Walsing Winning Trick of Edgerstoune emulated Pattern and also gained the pinnacle at Westminster (1950).'

Mrs John Marvin bred three Best in Show Westies, a wonderful accomplishment for any breeder, and she has been actively in the dog show scene for over half a century. Her husband John Marvin was a well-known terrier writer and both Marvins were judges of many breeds. John and Bea loved England and made yearly trips to the British Isles, watching the judging, looking over the dogs, searching out dog books and visiting with their many friends.

Wishing Well Kennels, started by Mrs Florence Worcester and her daughter Barbara Keenan, began about 1950. Barbara purchased her first Westie at the age of 13 from Mrs Winant of Edgerstoune Kennels. In 1954, she imported Ch Cruben Dexter, who became a leading sire as well as a Best in Show dog. Her import, Ch Elfinbrook Simon, not fully appreciated in his home country, went Best in Show at Westminster in 1962 and added 26 more Bests in Show to his name in addition to being an influence as a sire in the breed. Dogs and bitches from this kennel have been a force in the Westie world in America for many years. Mrs Keenan is also a very well-known judge.

Naomi and Jim Eberhardt were active breeders and exhibitors for many years. They have had approximately 75 American Westie champions, have been active in the breed club, and both judge numerous breeds. Many years ago I attended my first Montgomery County show in Pennsylvania and the weather was very cold and wet. (I have since learned that these can be prevalent weather conditions for this show, similar to most of the shows in England.) Mr Eberhardt gave me some wonderful little handwarmers that campers used. I put them in my pocket and thought that he had saved my day, in addition to probably saving my life! Of course, I admired the Americans for having these clever products and for being smart

Miss Genevieve Tobin, a famous film star of her day, and her smiling West Highland White Terrier named Punch. Miss Tobin was very influential in the popularisation of the breed.

enough to bring them to a dog show.

There have been many active breeders of Westies in America and books authored by John Marvin and Anna Katherine Nicholas give extensive history of the breed in the U.S.

WESTIES IN CANADA

In Canada the first Westie registered was a bitch in 1909. Victor Blochin, Bencruachan Kennels, owned the first Group-winning Westie in Canada. He bred from the 1930s to the 1950s and his dogs are found in the background of many Canadian kennels,

---

DID YOU KNOW?

Records dating back to James I (1566—1675) note that he requested that '6 little white earth dogs from Argyllshire be sent to the King of France as a gift.' Are these the ancestors of the modern Westie? Sir Edwin Landseer's 'Dignity and Impudence,' 1839, shows a hound and a small white Terrier that is undoubtedly a West Highland White Terrier.

A West Highland White bitch and her puppies, photographed in the 1920s. Note the considerable similarities in type between this dam and many of today's Westies.

including the kennel of Mrs J H Daniell-Jenkins.

Mr and Mrs Daniell-Jenkins' Kennels of The Rouge was a very active kennel, founded in 1948. Mrs Jenkins worked closely with Mrs B G Frame of the Wiston Kennels in the U.S. She was a very busy and popular dog show judge throughout North America where an exhibitor always knew that she would look over the dog competently and carefully. She passed away in 1992.

Penny-Belle Scorer has had Westies for most of her life. Mrs Daniell-Jenkins invited her for a

Mrs Pacey was famous in Scotland for her Wolvey kennel, which produced a very uniform variety of Westie. This photograph was taken in 1909, in the first decade of the breed.

Eleven of the Poltalloch dogs of Col. Malcolm. From these dogs derive most of the West Highland White Terriers in the world today!

West Highland White Terrier puppies born in America about 1920. The breed grew in popularity on both sides of the Atlantic.

visit to see the Kennels of The Rouge Westies and later Penny-Belle became a member of the West Highland White Terrier Club of England under the auspices of Mrs Jenkins. Her first import was Ch Arnholme Almost an Angel, who has more than 20 champion descendants. Her Can. and Am. Ch Biljon Bisbee finished his title in one week and became Canada's #2 Westie and #5 Terrier in 1984. In 1985 she imported Brierlaw Blaze a Trail who became #1 Westie in Canada in 1986, 1987 and 1988. He not only earned his Canadian Championship but also added American and Bermuda championships to his name.

WESTIES AROUND THE WORLD
Westies were first shown in Australia in 1964. During the 1960s dogs were imported from England, including some Wolvey dogs. Australia has a group of dedicated breeders with good dogs and the future of the breed 'Down Under' is in good hands.
　　Westies have become popular

in the Scandinavian countries also. Barbro Eklund introduced Westies to her Swedish Kennel of Scottish Terriers. In 1962 Birgitta Hasselgren bought her first Westie from Mrs Eklund and this was the start of the Tweed Kennels. Her

DID YOU KNOW?
The Cairn Terrier and the West Highland White Terrier closely resemble each other. The early Cairn breeders were very careful not to keep Cairn puppies that had any white in their coats and any puppies that did have white were culled at birth. On the other hand, the breeders of the white terriers made certain that their dogs were completely white. Interbreeding of the two breeds continued until 1917 when the American Kennel Club stated that no Cairn could be registered if there was a Westie cross within the first three generations. The Kennel Club followed suit shortly after.

Almost 100 years ago West Highland Whites and Cairns were used almost exclusively in Scotland as rodent killers. Their owner, Miss Ransford, credited these three hunters with killing 101 rats in six nights!

European-bred West Highland White Terriers are vivacious and intelligent as is confirmed by the expressions on the faces of these dogs.

Eng. Swed. Ch Tweed Tartan Caledonia has sired many Swedish and English champions. Louise Westerberg from Smash Kennels has also produced top winners. Swed. Ch Smash Scallyway was #3 Terrier in Sweden in 1989. Swed. Ch Smash Turbo was the #1 Westie in 1991 and a multiple Best in Show winner.

Westies have been in Finland since the 1930s but the breed became very popular in the 1980s with membership in the Westie club growing to over 400. In the 1960s, Ch Wolvey Proton was imported by Marita Palmo and her name appears in many pedigrees, even up to the 1980s. Registrations reached record numbers in the 1970s but registrations began to decline in the 1980s. Once again in the 1990s, the breed flourished with many active and dedicated breeders.

In Norway, the first Westie was imported from England in 1931. In 1984 Olac Moon Falcon was imported and became a multiple Group and Best in Show winner. The Norwegian Westie Club, an unofficial club, has over 175 members and in 1989 the breed had 191 registrations, including 23 imports. Although the numbers are still small in

Norway, the breed is increasing in popularity.

Derek Tattersall, of the very successful Olac Kennels in England, has an interest in the breed in the Scandinavian countries and has written in depth about this in his book *Westies Today.*

The West Highland White Terrier, in less than 100 years, has become a very beloved breed throughout the world. It continues to be in good hands from North

Today's Westie has found many other uses for his talents. Agility trials have been popular in Britain for many years and are becoming widespread around the world.

America to the Continent to Australia. England continues to be its home but top dogs are now coming from around the world.

From their origins in Scotland about a century ago, today's handsome West Highland White Terrier has become recognised and adored around the world.

If you are Scottish, you'll know what this is all about. Scottish clans have regular annual outings during which they sport their traditional garb and show off their national dogs.

CHARACTERISTICS OF THE
West Highland White Terrier

The Westie is a wonderful little dog! He's cute, 'flat'-sized, filled with personality-plus and very active. Some terriers, like the Westie, are 'below the knee' in size, but in spite of their size, all terriers are masculine dogs and do not show any sign of timidity or shyness. These are busy dogs, on their toes and ready for action! If you are looking for a sedentary lap dog, this will not be the breed for you.

The Westie has a very steady disposition and fits in well with family life, whether it be in a large country house or a flat in the city. He gets along well with children and will accept strangers once he has had a chance to become acquainted. He's a cocky dog who may not go out and start a fight but he will surely stand his ground when pushed. This is not a dog that will lay about the house trying to keep his master or mistress happy. He has been bred as a hunter, a dog to go after vermin, and he can be ready to work instantly.

Common characteristics for all terriers are their desire to work with great enthusiasm and courage. They all have large and powerful teeth for the size of their bodies; they have keen hearing and excellent eyesight. No matter for how many generations they have been pets, the purpose for which the breed was bred will remain with the dog.

The Westie is similar to his Scottish counterparts, the Scottish Terrier and the Cairn Terrier. Of the three, the Scottie is the most substantial dog, the heaviest in weight, the largest in bone and the

Most Westies today live in pet homes, keeping their masters and mistresses warm and happy.

23

most dour in personality. The Cairn is the lightweight of the group, being a small-boned and lightly built animal. The Westie is nicely placed between these two breeds, in substance and personality. He has substantial bone but weighs less than the Scottie. He likes to have a good time but he is steady in his personality. He likes to please his keepers and has a happy outlook on life. Take a look at a Westie and you can see the sparkle in his eye that says, 'Come play with me!' He is a quick, alert, and intelligent dog who likes his owner to be his equal.

If you are a first-time dog owner you must be aware of your

DID YOU KNOW?

Do you want to live longer? If you like to volunteer, it is wonderful if you can take your Westie to a nursing home once a week for several hours. The elder community loves to have a dog to visit with and often your dog will bring a bit of companionship to someone who is either lonely or who may be somewhat detached from the world. You will not only be bringing happiness to someone else, but you will be keeping your little dog busy—and we haven't even mentioned the fact that they have discovered that volunteering helps to increase your longevity!

responsibility toward your new friend. Either keep your dog on a leash or in your fenced yard. Your Westie, if loose and trotting along at your side, will spot a squirrel across a busy street and dart after it, never minding the traffic. Therefore, some rudimentary obedience training should be in line so your chum will sit when asked to, come when called and, in general, act like a little gentleman.

Westies, as with other terriers, can be a challenge in the obedience ring. Terriers are not an easy breed to work with in obedience. Their intelligence and independent spirit can sometimes be more trying to train than most owners anticipate. You will see Golden

Westies love to be petted. It is not unusual that they will lie on their backs and expose their soft underbelly to be scratched. This is the ultimate posture of submission.

First, there is the problem of a white dog. White dogs will show the wear and tear of their busy lives. Scotties, with their dark coats, and Cairns, with their mottled coats, can run up and down the garden and when you bring them in you may not be aware of just how soiled their coats may be. The Westie, on the other hand, particularly if he has been digging, which terriers are prone to do, will truly look a sight as he runs through the door on your clean kitchen floor. If it is a wet and muddy day, he will look even more frightful. Grooming, a requirement in all breeds, is essential in the Westie if you want a dog that you can live with.

Second, there are health problems in most breeds of dogs and the West Highland Terrier is no

Retrievers, Poodles and Miniature Schnauzers in abundance in obedience classes as these are breeds that are easy to work with. Not only are they intelligent, but more importantly, they have a willingness to please their master, a quality that is less abundant in the terrier breeds.

The terrier is easily distracted and busy but he is an intelligent dog and he does respond to training. Of course, when training a smart and independent dog, the handler will often learn humility whilst the dog is learning his sits and stays.

As desirable as the Westie sounds, do be aware when purchasing this breed that there are some problems that you do not have in other breeds.

DID YOU KNOW?

Westie Foundation of America, Inc., is an arm of the West Highland Terrier Club of America. This is a foundation supported by the national club, its regional clubs and its membership. Financial assistance is given for medical research of health problems in the Westie. Findings will help breeders of Westies throughout the world and will give all the hope that some of the breed's health problems will eventually be eliminated.

A responsible owner must learn about the possible problems that Westies encounter and what can be done to safeguard his or her pet.

exception. The new Westie owner should be aware of these problems. Do remember to buy your puppy from a reputable breeder and ask the breeder if any of these health problems are in her line.

Legge-Calve-Perthes disease (Perthes) is a bone related disease that affects short-legged terriers as well as humans. This is not a hereditary disease and it is thought to be caused by an injury or possibly a nutritional problem. The disease appears between four and ten

Youngsters must learn to properly hold and play with the Westie puppy. Vets suggest that many physical problems can be caused by improper handling.

between the lower jaw and the skull, a multiplication in growth of bone cells. It usually occurs between four and seven months and it must not be confused with a teething problem or with cancer. Puppies who have this disease will have difficulty in opening their mouths. Diagnosis is made by x-ray and cortisone, and homoeopathic remedies have been used

months and is very painful. The dog will limp on one or both rear legs and eventually the leg muscles become wasted. There are some treatments for Perthes that should be discussed with your veterinary surgeon.

Craniomandibular osteopathy (CMO) is a fairly rare disease found in Westies, Scotties and Cairns. It is apparently an hereditary disease although the exact pattern of inheritance is not known. This is a calcification of the joint

DID YOU KNOW?
Eczema and dermatitis are skin problems that occur in many breeds and they can often be a tricky problem to solve. Frequent bathing of the dog will remove skin oils and will cause the problem to worsen. Allergies to food or something in the environment, can also cause the problem. Consider trying homeopathic remedies in addition to seeing your veterinarian for direction.

with good results. This is a very painful disease for the dog.

Copper toxicosis is a serious problem in the Bedlington Terrier and has been found in some bloodlines in Westies. Affected animals develop hepatitis and eventually liver cirrhosis. Considerable studies and testing have been done on this problem and researchers have found that the disease is caused by an autosomal recessive gene that results in faulty copper excretion from the liver. Reputable breeders will have their dogs tested and will not breed to or from infected dogs.

Keratoconjunctivitis sicca (dry eye) is a problem that was noticed in Westies in the early 1980s. This is not a common problem in the breed, but it has been reported and owners and breeders should be aware of it. It is a recurrent form of

Westies are usually happy, healthy dogs that make great pets. They should, however, be taken to a vet every year for a general physical examination. Many maladies, if detected and treated early, can be successfully cured.

Keep your eye on your Westie's eyes. The might develop conjunctivitis, which usually can be successfully treated by a veterinary surgeon.

conjunctivitis that becomes chronic and very painful for the dog. The problem can be treated with drugs that will increase the secretion of tears but this is not a long-term solution.

Although this list of health problems may look daunting, Westies are still considered to be a healthy breed. The problems mentioned are in the breed and a buyer should be aware of them. Some of these diseases are rare and most of them only turn up on the rare occasion. Do not be turned away from the breed but do be aware that if the breeder of your puppy is reputable and aware of these problems, she will be doing her utmost to keep them out of her line.

WORKING TRIALS FOR TERRIERS

In the U.S., the American Working Terrier Association offers a Certificate of Gameness at sanctioned trials. A dog must enter a 10-foot-long tunnel buried in the ground, which includes one right-angle turn. Once in the tunnel, he must reach his prey in 30 seconds. Working Trials are held throughout the country and open to all terriers.

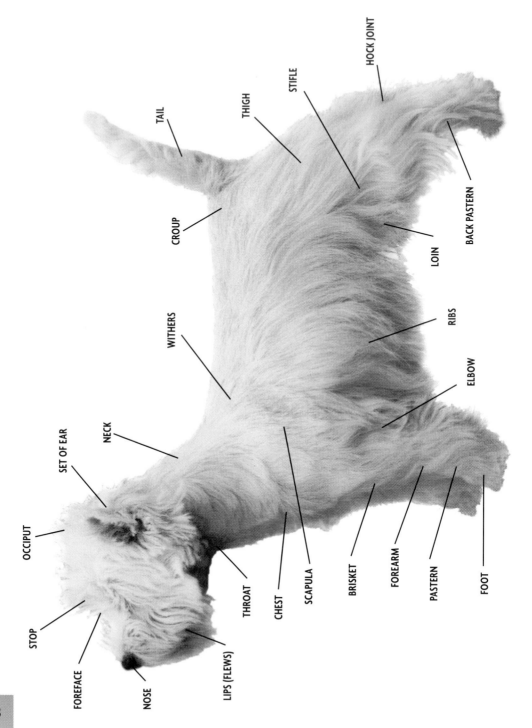

TAIL

THIGH

STIFLE

HOCK JOINT

CROUP

BACK PASTERN

LOIN

WITHERS

RIBS

ELBOW

SET OF EAR

NECK

OCCIPUT

STOP

FOREFACE

NOSE

THROAT

CHEST

SCAPULA

BRISKET

FOREARM

PASTERN

FOOT

LIPS (FLEWS)

West Highland White Terrier

Each breed approved by The Kennel Club has a standard that gives the reader a mental picture of what the specific breed should look like. All reputable breeders strive to produce animals that will meet the requirements of the standard. Most breeds were developed for a specific purpose, i.e., hunting, retrieving, going to ground, coursing, guarding, herding, etc. The terriers were all bred to go to ground and to pursue vermin.

West Highland White Terriers, like many breeds, have evolved over the years. Compared to early representatives of the breed, today's Westies are more refined and impressive.

In addition to having dogs that look like proper West Highland White Terriers, the standard assures that the Westie will have the personality, disposition and intelligence that are sought after in the breed.

Standards were originally written by fanciers who had a love and a concern for the breed. They knew that the essential characteristics of the West Highland White Terrier were unlike any other breed and that care must be taken that these characteristics be maintained through the generations.

As time progressed and breeders became more aware that certain areas of the dog needed a better description or more definition, breeders would meet together and work out a new

Many points in a breed standard are subject to interpretation. In the Westie standard, there can be no discussion of 'Colour: White.'

standard. However, standards for any breed are never changed on a whim and serious study and exchange between breeders takes place before any move is made. In England, The Kennel Club, the governing body of the dog world, controls all breed standards and determines when alterations should be instituted.

THE KENNEL CLUB STANDARD FOR THE WEST HIGHLAND WHITE TERRIER

General Appearance: Strongly built; deep in chest and back ribs; level back and powerful quarters on muscular legs and exhibiting in a marked degree a great combination of strength and activity.

Characteristics: Small, active, game, hardy, possessed of no small amount of self-esteem with a varminty appearance.

Temperament: Alert, gay, courageous, self-reliant but friendly.

Head and Skull: Skull slightly domed; when handled across forehead presents a smooth contour. Tapering very slightly from skull at level of ears to eyes. Distance from occiput to eyes slightly greater than length of foreface. Head thickly coated with hair, and carried at right angle or less, to axis of neck. Head not to be carried in extended position. Foreface gradually tapering from eye to muzzle.

This lovely West Highland White Terrier is a Group winner from Ireland. What a fine specimen and a handsome coat!

The correct head on the West Highland White Terrier imparts the breed with a distinctive look. The breed should appear absolutely dignified, courageous and gay.

Distinct stop formed by heavy, bony ridges immediately above and slightly overhanging eye, and slight indentation between eyes. Foreface not dished nor falling away quickly below eyes, where it is well made up. Jaws strong and level. Nose black and fairly large, forming smooth contour with rest of muzzle. Nose not projecting forward.

Eyes: Set wide apart, medium in size, not full, as dark as possible. Slightly sunk in head, sharp and intelligent, which, looking from under heavy eyebrows, imparts a piercing look. Light coloured eyes highly undesirable.

Ears: Small, erect and carried firmly, terminating in sharp point, set neither too wide nor too close. Hair short and smooth (velvety), should not be cut. Free from any fringe at top. Round-pointed, broad, large or thick ears or too heavily coated with hair most undesirable.

Mouth: As broad between canine teeth as is consistent with varminty expression required. Teeth large for size of dog, with regular scissors bite, i.e., upper teeth closely overlapping lower teeth and set square to the jaws.

Neck: Sufficiently long to allow

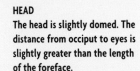

HEAD

The head is slightly domed. The distance from occiput to eyes is slightly greater than the length of the foreface.

EARS

The ears should be small, erect and pointed (left). They should not be rounded and set too wide apart (right).

BACK AND NECK

The back is level and the shoulder should slope backwards (left). The neck is sufficiently long but never exaggerated as shown on the right.

HINDQUARTERS

The hocks are bent and well set in under the body (left). Weak hocks and cow hocks (turning inward) are undesirable (right).

FOREQUARTERS

The forelegs are straight and muscular (left), never turning out at the elbows (right).

proper set on of head required, muscular and gradually thickening toward base allowing neck to merge into nicely sloping shoulders.

Forequarters: Shoulders sloping backwards. Shoulder blades broad and lying close to chest wall. Shoulder joint placed forward, elbows well in, allowing foreleg to move freely, parallel to axis of body. Forelegs short and muscular, straight and thickly covered with short, hard hair.

Body: Compact. Back level, loins broad and strong. Chest deep and ribs well arched in upper half presenting a flattish side appearance. Back ribs of considerable depth and distance from last rib of quarters as short as compatible with free movement of body.

Hindquarters: Strong, muscular and wide across top. Legs short, muscular and sinewy. Thighs very muscular and not too wide apart. Hocks bent and well set in under body so as to be fairly close to each other when standing or moving. Straight or weak hocks most undesirable.

Feet: Forefeet larger than hind, round, proportionate in size, strong, thickly padded and covered with short harsh hair. Hindfeet are smaller and thickly padded. Under surface of pads and all nails preferably black.

Tail: 12.5–15 cms (5–6 ins) long, covered with harsh hair, no feathering, as straight as possible, carried jauntily, not gay or carried over back. A long tail undesirable, and on no account should tails be docked.

Gait/Movement: Free, straight and easy all round. In front, legs freely extended forward from shoulder. Hind movement free, strong and close. Stifle and hocks well flexed and hocks drawn under body giving drive. Stiff, stilted movement behind and cowhocks highly undesirable.

Coat: Double coated. Outer coat consists of harsh hair, about 5 cms (2 ins) long, free from any curl. Undercoat, which resembles fur, short, soft and close. Open coats most undesirable.

Colour: White.

Size: Height at withers approximately 28 cms (11 ins).

Faults: Any departure from the foregoing points should be considered a fault and the seriousness with which the fault should be regarded should be in exact proportion to its degree.

Note: Male animals should have two apparently normal testicles fully descended into the scrotum.

Dogs like the West Highland White Terrier are bred to preserve their physical characteristics, described in the breed standard, as well as such intangible properties as personality and temperament.

West Highland White Terrier

WHERE TO BEGIN?

If you are convinced that the West Highland White Terrier is the ideal dog for you, it's time to learn about where to find a puppy and what to look for. Locating a litter of Westies should not present a problem for the new owner. You should inquire about breeders in your area who enjoy a good reputation in the breed. You are looking for an established breeder with outstanding dog ethics and a strong commitment to the breed. New owners should have as many questions as they have doubts. An established breeder is indeed the one to answer your four million questions and make you comfortable with your choice of the West

The price you pay for a puppy is usually related to the quality of the parents. Puppies bred from champion West Highland White Terriers promise to be the healthiest and closest to the breed standard.

Highland White Terrier. An established breeder will sell you a puppy at a fair price if, and only if, the breeder determines that you are a suitable, worthy owner of his/her dogs. An established breeder can be relied upon for advice, no matter what time of day or night. A reputable breeder will accept a puppy back, without questions, should you decide that this is not the right dog for you.

When choosing a breeder, reputation is much more important than convenience of location. Do not be overly impressed by breeders who run brag advertisements in the presses about their stupendous champions and working lines. The real quality breeders are quiet and unassuming. You hear about them

When observing a litter of West Highland White Terrier puppies, select a puppy that is animated and affectionate. Never feel sorry for the puppies that shy away from you.

37

Although most breeders will not allow potential customers to visit the litter when it's this young, you should be able to visit the litter by four or five weeks, sometimes later.

at the dog trials and shows, by word of mouth. You may be well advised to avoid the novice who lives only a couple miles away. The local novice breeder, trying so hard to get rid of that first litter of puppies, is more than accommodating and anxious to sell you one. That breeder will charge you as much as any established breeder. The novice breeder isn't going to interrogate you and your family about your intentions with the puppy, the environment and training you can provide, etc. That breeder will be nowhere to be found when your poorly bred, badly adjusted four-pawed monster starts to growl and spit up at midnight or eat the family cat!

Whilst health considerations in the West Highland White Terrier are not nearly as daunting as in many other breeds, socialisation is a breeder concern of considerable importance. Since the West Highland White Terrier's temperament can vary from line to line, socialisation is the first and best way to encourage a

proper, stable personality.

Choosing a breeder is an important first step in dog ownership. Fortunately, the majority of Westie breeders are devoted to the breed and its well being. New owners should have little problem finding a reputable breeder who doesn't live on the other side of the country (or in a different country). The Kennel Club is able to recommend breeders of quality West Highland White Terriers, as can any local all-breed club or Westie club. Potential owners are encouraged to attend a dog show to meet the handlers firsthand and to get an idea what West Highland White Terriers look like outside of a photographer's lens. Provided you

DID YOU KNOW?
Breeders rarely release puppies until they are eight to ten weeks of age. This is an acceptable age for most breeds of dog, excepting toy breeds which are not released until around 12 weeks, given their petite sizes. If a breeder has a puppy that is 12 weeks or more, it is likely well socialised and housetrained. Be sure that it is otherwise healthy before deciding to take it home.

the breeder doesn't have any waiting list, or any customers, there is probably a good reason. It's no different than visiting a pub with no clientele. The better pubs and restaurants always have a waiting list—-and it's usually worth the wait. Besides, isn't a puppy more important than a pint?

Since you are likely choosing a West Highland White Terrier as a pet dog and not as a show dog, you simply should select a pup that is friendly and attractive. Whilst the basic structure of the breed has little variation, the temperament may present trouble in certain strains. Beware of the shy or overly aggressive puppy: be

At this Scottish-Irish festival, many British breeds are on display, and it is a good opportunity to meet dogs and their owners. These festivals are common in America.

approach the handlers when they are not terribly busy with the dogs, most are more than willing to answer questions, recommend breeders and give advice.

Now that you have contacted and met a breeder or two and made your choice about which breeder is best suited to your needs, it's time to visit the litter. Keep in mind that many top breeders have waiting lists. Sometimes new owners have to wait as long as two years for a puppy. If you are really committed to the breeder whom you've selected, then you will wait (and hope for an early arrival!). If not, you may have to resort to your second or third choice breeder. Don't be too anxious, however. If

especially conscious of the nervous West Highland White Terrier pup. Don't let sentiment or emotion trap you into buying the runt of the litter.

The gender of your puppy is largely a matter of personal taste, although there is a common belief amongst fanciers that bitches are quicker to learn and generally

Your breeder should be able to show you the dam's bite if you are concerned about the puppy's mouth. This adult possesses the desired scissors bite.

more loving and faithful. Males learn more slowly but retain the lesson longer. The difference in size is noticeable but slight.

Breeders commonly allow visitors to see the litter by around the fifth or sixth week, and puppies leave for their new homes between the eighth and tenth week. Breeders who permit their puppies to leave early are more interested in your pounds than their puppies' well being.

DID YOU KNOW?

An important consideration to be discussed is the sex of your puppy. For a family companion, a bitch may be the better choice, considering the female's inbred concern for all young creatures and her accompanying tolerance and patience. It is always advised to spay a pet bitch, which may guarantee her a longer life.

Puppies need to learn the rules of the trade from their dams, and most dams continue teaching the pups manners and dos and don'ts until around the eighth week. Breeders spend significant amounts of time with the Westie

DID YOU KNOW?

Your selection of a good puppy can be determined by your needs. A show potential or a good pet? It is your choice. Every puppy, however, should be of good temperament. Although show-quality puppies are bred and raised with emphasis on physical conformation, responsible breeders strive for equally good temperament. Do not buy from a breeder who concentrates solely on physical beauty at the expense of personality.

You should be so lucky as to have a litter as frisky and alert as this one from which to choose your new Westie! Select the puppy with the personality and energy that appeals to you.

toddlers so that they are able to interact with the 'other species,' i.e., humans. Given the long history that dogs and humans have, bonding between the two species is natural but must be nurtured. A well-bred, well-socialised West Highland White Terrier pup wants nothing more than to be near you and please you.

Always check the bite of your selected puppy to be sure that it is neither overshot or undershot. This may not be too noticeable on a young puppy but it is important to check for overall soundness.

COMMITMENT OF OWNERSHIP

After considering all of these factors, you have most likely already made some very important decisions about selecting your puppy. You have chosen a West Highland White Terrier, which means that you have decided which characteristics you want in a dog and what type of dog will best fit into your family and lifestyle. If you have selected a breeder, you have gone a step further—you have done your research and found a responsible, conscientious person who breeds quality West Highland White Terriers and who should be a reliable source of help as you and your puppy adjust to life together. If you have observed a litter in action, you have obtained a firsthand look at the dynamics of a puppy 'pack' and, thus, you should learn about each pup's individual personality—perhaps you have even found one that particularly appeals to you.

However, even if you have not yet found the West Highland White Terrier puppy of your dreams, observing pups will help

DID YOU KNOW?

Training your puppy takes much patience and can be frustrating at times, but you should see results from your efforts. If you have a puppy that seems untrainable, take him to a trainer or behaviourist. The dog may have a personality problem that requires the help of a professional, or perhaps you need help in learning how to train your dog.

you learn to recognise certain behaviour and to determine what a pup's behaviour indicates about his temperament. You will be able to pick out which pups are the leaders, which ones are less outgoing, which ones are confident, which ones are shy, playful, friendly, aggressive, etc. Equally as important, you will learn to recognise what a healthy pup should look and act like. All of these things will help you in your search, and when you find the West Highland White Terrier that was meant for you, you will know it!

Researching your breed, selecting a responsible breeder and observing as many pups as possible are all important steps on the way to dog ownership. It may seem like a lot of effort...and you have not even brought the pup home yet! Remember, though, you

DID YOU KNOW?

If you lead an erratic, unpredictable life, with daily or weekly changes in your work requirements, consider the problems of owning a puppy. The new puppy has to be fed regularly, socialised (loved, petted, handled, introduced to other people) and, most importantly, allowed to visit outdoors for toilet training. As the dog gets older, it can be more tolerant of deviations in its feeding and toilet relief.

ornament, but a creature that will become a real member of your family. You will come to realise that, whilst buying a puppy is a pleasurable and exciting endeavour, it is not something to be taken lightly. Relax…the fun will start when the pup comes home!

Always keep in mind that a puppy is nothing more than a

cannot be too careful when it comes to deciding on the type of dog you want and finding out about your prospective pup's background. Buying a puppy is not—or should not be—just another whimsical purchase. This is one instance in which you actually do get to choose your own family! You may be thinking that buying a puppy should be fun—it should not be so serious and so much work. Keep in mind that your puppy is not a cuddly stuffed toy or decorative lawn

As anxious and curious as your Westie puppy is, do not let it run unattended through the garden. A puppy is virtually helpless in the human world and relies upon you for protection.

baby in a furry disguise…a baby who is virtually helpless in a human world and who trusts his owner for fulfilment of his basic needs for survival. In addition to water and shelter, your pup needs care, protection, guidance and love. If you are not prepared to commit to this, then you are not prepared to own a dog.

Wait a minute, you say. How hard could this be? All of my neighbours own dogs and they seem to be doing just fine. Why should I have to worry about all of this? Well, you should not worry about it; in fact, you will probably find that once your West Highland White Terrier pup gets used to his new home, he will fall into his place in the family quite naturally. But it never hurts to emphasise the commitment of dog

DID YOU KNOW?

The majority of problems that are commonly seen in young pups will disappear as your dog gets older. However, how you deal with problems when he is young will determine how he reacts to discipline as an adult dog. It is important to establish who is boss (hopefully it will be you!) right away when you are first bonding with your dog. This bond will set the tone for the rest of your life together.

ownership. With some time and patience, it is really not too difficult to raise a curious and exuberant West Highland White Terrier pup to be a well-adjusted and well-mannered adult dog—a dog that could be your most loyal friend.

PREPARING PUPPY'S PLACE IN YOUR HOME

Researching your breed and finding a breeder are only two aspects of the 'homework' you will have to do before bringing your West Highland White Terrier puppy home. You will also have to prepare your home and family for the new addition. Much like you would prepare a nursery for a newborn baby, you will need to designate a place in your home that will be the puppy's own. How you prepare your home will

DID YOU KNOW?

You will probably start feeding your pup the same food that he has been getting from the breeder; the breeder should give you a few days' supply to start you off. Although you should not give your pup too many treats, you will want to have puppy treats on hand for coaxing, training, rewards, etc. Be careful, though, as a small pup's calorie requirements are relatively low and a few treats can add up to almost a full day's worth of calories without the required nutrition.

depend on how much freedom the dog will be allowed. Will he be confined to one room or a specific area in the house, or will he be allowed to roam as he pleases? Will he spend most of his time in the house or will he be primarily an outdoor dog? Whatever you decide, you must ensure that he has a place that he can 'call his own.'

When you bring your new puppy into your home, you are bringing him into what will become his home as well. Obviously, you did not buy a puppy so that he could take over your house, but in order for a puppy to grow into a stable, well-adjusted dog, he has to feel comfortable in his surroundings. Remember, he is leaving the warmth and security of his mother and littermates, as well as the familiarity of the only place he has ever known, so it is important to make his transition as easy as possible. By preparing a place in your home for the puppy, you are making him feel as welcome as possible in a strange new place. It should not take him long to get used to it, but the sudden shock of being transplanted is somewhat traumatic for a young pup. Imagine how a small child would feel in the same situation—that is how your puppy must be feeling. It is up to you to reassure him and to let him know, 'Little fellow, you are going to like it here!'

Be prepared for your pup's arrival. Ask your veterinary surgeon to recommend the equipment you will need.

DID YOU KNOW?

During crate training, you should partition off the section of the crate in which the pup stays. If he is given too big an area, this will hinder your training efforts. Crate training is based on the fact that a dog does not like to soil his sleeping quarters, so it is ineffective to keep a pup in a crate that is so big that he can eliminate in one end and get far enough away from it to sleep. Also, you want to make the crate den-like for the pup. Blankets and a favourite toy will make the crate cosy for the small pup; as he grows, you may want to evict some of his 'roommates' to make more room.

It will take some coaxing at first, but be patient. Given some time to get used to it, your pup will adapt to his new home-within-a-home quite nicely.

Your local pet shop can offer many types and sizes of kennels.

PHOTO COURTESY OF DOSKOCIL.

WHAT YOU SHOULD BUY
CRATE

To someone unfamiliar with the use of crates in dog training, it may seem like punishment to shut a dog in a crate, but this is not the case at all. Crates are not cruel—crates have many humane and highly effective uses in dog care and training. For example, crate training is a very popular and very successful housebreaking method. A crate can keep your dog safe during travel; and, perhaps most importantly, a crate provides your dog with a place of his own in your home. It serves as a 'doggie bedroom' of sorts— your West Highland White Terrier can curl up in his crate when he wants to sleep or when he just needs a break. Many dogs sleep in their crates overnight. When lined with soft blankets and a favourite toy, a crate becomes a cosy pseudo-den for your dog. Like his ancestors, he too will seek out the comfort and retreat of a den—you just happen to be providing him with something a little more luxurious than leaves and twigs lining a dirty ditch.

As far as purchasing a crate, the type that you buy is up to you. It will most likely be one of the two most popular types: wire or fibreglass. There are advantages and disadvantages to each type. For example, a wire crate is more open, allowing the air to flow through and affording the dog a view of what is going on around him. A fibreglass crate, however, is sturdier and can double as a travel crate since it provides more protection for the dog. The size of the crate is another thing to consider. Puppies do not stay puppies forever—in fact, sometimes it seems as if they grow right before your eyes. A Yorkie-sized crate may be fine for a very young West Highland White Terrier pup, but it will not do him much good for long! Unless you have the money and the inclination to buy a new crate every time your pup has a growth spurt, it is better to get one that will accommodate your dog both as a pup and at full size.

BEDDING

Veterinary bedding in the dog's crate will help the dog feel more at home and you may pop in a small blanket. First, the bedding will take the place of the leaves, twigs, etc., that the pup would use in the wild to make a den; the pup can make his own 'burrow' in the crate. Although your pup is far removed from his den-making ancestors, the denning instinct is still a part of his genetic makeup. Second, until you bring your pup home, he has been sleeping amidst the warmth of his mother and litter-mates, and whilst a blanket is not the same as a warm, breathing body, it still provides heat and something with which to snuggle. You will want to wash your pup's blankets frequently in case he has an accident in his crate, and replace or remove any blanket that becomes ragged and starts to fall apart.

TOYS

Toys are a must for dogs of all ages, especially for curious playful pups. Puppies are the 'children' of the dog world, and what child does not love toys?

Westies love to have a bed of their own with a soft blanket. The bedding should be washed frequently as the dog may soil it with his feet.

Chew toys provide enjoyment to both dog and owner—your dog will enjoy playing with his favourite toys, whilst you will enjoy the fact

DID YOU KNOW?

With a big variety of dog toys available, and so many that look like they would be a lot of fun for a dog, be careful in your selection. It is amazing what a set of puppy teeth can do to an innocent-looking toy, so, obviously, safety is a major consideration. Be sure to choose the most durable products that you can find. Hard nylon bones and toys are a safe bet, and many of them are offered in different scents and flavours that will be sure to capture your dog's attention. It is always fun to play a game of catch with your dog, and there are balls and flying discs that are specially made to withstand dog teeth.

You will need different kinds of dog toys for chewing, exercise and entertainment. Be careful! Poorly made toys can be very dangerous as Westies can easily chew them apart and swallow the pieces.

DID YOU KNOW?

Grooming tools, collars, leashes, dog beds and, of course, toys will be an expense to you when you first obtain your pup, and the cost will trickle on throughout your dog's lifetime. If your puppy damages or destroys your possessions (as most puppies surely will!) or something belonging to a neighbour, you can calculate additional expense. There is also flea and pest control, which every dog owner faces more than once. You must be able to handle the financial responsibility of owning a dog.

that they distract him from your expensive shoes and leather sofa. Puppies love to chew; in fact, chewing is a physical need for pups as they are teething, and everything looks appetising! The full range of your possessions—from old dishrag to Oriental rug—are fair game in the eyes of a teething pup. Puppies are not all that discerning when it comes to finding something to literally 'sink their teeth into'— everything tastes great!

West Highland White Terrier puppies are fairly aggressive chewers, as is true of most of the terrier breeds. Breeders advise owners to resist stuffed toys, because they can become destuffed in no time. The overly excited pup may ingest the stuffing, which is neither digestible nor nutritious.

Similarly, squeaky toys are quite popular, but should be avoided for the West Highland White Terrier. Perhaps a squeaky toy can be used as an aid in training, but not for free play. If a pup 'disembowels' one of these, the small plastic squeaker inside can be dangerous if swallowed. Monitor the condition of all your pup's toys carefully and get rid of any that have been chewed to the point of becoming potentially dangerous.

Be careful of natural bones, which have a tendency to splinter into sharp, dangerous pieces. Also be careful of rawhide, which can turn into

Your local pet shop usually carries a very complete selection of leads.

pieces that are easy to swallow or into a mushy mess on your carpet.

LEAD

A nylon lead is probably the best option as it is the most resistant to puppy teeth should your pup take a liking to chewing on his lead. Of course, this is a habit that should be nipped in the bud, but if your pup likes to chew on his lead he has a very slim chance of being able to chew through the strong nylon. Nylon leads are also lightweight, which is good for a young West Highland White Terrier who is just getting used to the idea of walking on a lead. For

Westie puppies must chew. Soft toys, besides being expensive and easily destroyed, can be dangerous should the puppy swallow bits and pieces.

49

everyday walking and safety purposes, the nylon lead is a good choice. As your pup grows up and gets used to walking on the lead, you may want to purchase a flexible lead. These leads allow you to extend the length to give the dog a broader area to explore or to shorten the length to keep the close to you.

COLLAR

Your pup should get used to wearing a collar all the time since you will want to attach his ID tags to it. You have to attach the lead to something! A lightweight nylon collar is a good choice; make sure that it fits snugly enough so that the pup cannot wriggle out of it, but is loose enough so that it will not be uncomfortably tight around the pup's neck. You should be able to fit a finger between the pup and the collar. It may take some time for your pup to get used to wearing the collar, but soon he will not even notice that it is there. Choke collars are made for training, but should only be used by an experienced handler.

FOOD AND WATER BOWLS

Your pup will need two bowls, one for food and one for water. You may want two sets of bowls, one for inside and one for outside, depending on where the dog will be fed and where he will be spending most of his time. Stainless steel or sturdy plastic bowls are popular choices. Plastic bowls are more chewable. Dogs tend not to chew on the steel variety, which can be sterilised. It is important to buy sturdy bowls since anything is in danger of being chewed by puppy teeth and you do not want your dog to be constantly chewing apart his bowl (for his safety and for your purse!).

CLEANING SUPPLIES

Until a pup is housetrained you will be doing a lot of cleaning. Accidents will occur, which is okay in the beginning because the puppy does not know any better. All you can do is be prepared to clean up any 'accidents.' Old rags, towels, newspapers and a safe disinfectant are good to have on hand.

It is better to supply your new Westie puppy with a safe chewable toy like a rawhide bone. Always supervise a young pup with any rawhide toys.

BEYOND THE BASICS

The items previously discussed are the bare necessities. You will find out what else you need as you go along—grooming supplies, flea/tick protection, baby gates to partition a room, etc. These things will vary depending on your situation but it is important that you have everything you need to feed and make your West Highland White Terrier comfortable in his first few days at home.

PUPPY-PROOFING YOUR HOME

Aside from making sure that your West Highland White Terrier will be comfortable in your home, you also have to make sure that your

Your local pet shop should have a variety of food and water bowls, or combinations thereof, made from metal, plastic and crockery.

NEVER fail to clean up your dog's bowel movements, even if they occur in your own garden. Your pet shop has accessories to assist you in this necessary task.

PHOTO COURTESY OF MIKKI PET PRODUCTS.

home is safe for your West Highland White Terrier. This means taking precautions that your pup will not get into anything he should not get into and that there is nothing within his reach that may harm him should he sniff it, chew it, inspect it, etc. This probably seems obvious since, whilst you are

Westie puppies are
very inquisitive.
Your garden
should be free of
plants that are
toxic or contain
herbicides, which
can be poisonous.
Flowers also
attract wasps and
bees, both of
which attack dogs
when provoked.

primarily concerned with your pup's safety, at the same time you do not want your belongings to be ruined. Breakables should be placed out of reach if your dog is to have full run of the house. If he is to be limited to certain places within the house, keep any potentially dangerous items in the 'off-limits' areas. An electrical cord can pose a danger should the puppy decide to taste it—and who is going to convince a pup that it would not make a great chew toy? Cords should be fastened tightly against the wall. If your dog is going to spend time in a crate, make sure that there is nothing near his crate that he can reach if he sticks his curious little nose or paws through the openings. Just as you would with a child, keep all household cleaners and chemicals where the pup cannot get to them.

It is also important to make sure that the outside of your home is safe. Of course your puppy should never be unsupervised, but a pup let loose in the garden will want to run and explore, and he should be granted that freedom. Do not let a fence give you a false sense of security; you would be surprised how crafty (and persistent) a dog can be in figuring out how to dig under and squeeze his way through small holes, or to jump or climb over a fence. The remedy is to make the fence high enough so that it really is impossible for your dog to get over it (about 3 metres should suffice), and well embedded into the ground. Be sure to repair or secure any gaps in the fence. Check the fence periodi-

DID YOU KNOW?

Many plants can be toxic to dogs. If you see your dog carrying a piece of vegetation in his mouth, approach him in a quiet, disinterested manner, avoid eye contact, pet him and gradually remove the plant from his mouth. Alternatively, offer him a treat and maybe he'll drop the plant on his own accord. Be sure no toxic plants are growing in your own garden.

FIRST TRIP TO THE VET

You have picked out your puppy, and your home and family are ready. Now all you have to do is collect your West Highland White Terrier from the breeder and the fun begins, right? Well...not so fast. Something else you need to prepare is your pup's first trip to the veterinary surgeon. Perhaps the breeder can recommend someone in the area that specialises in West Highland White Terriers, or maybe you know some

Your Westie's first visit to the vet will be an overall examination. Take your new dog to your veterinary surgeon as expeditiously as possible.

cally to ensure that it is in good shape and make repairs as needed; a very determined pup may return to the same spot to 'work on it' until he is able to get through. This is especially true with terrier breeds like your Westie.

other Westie owners who can suggest a good vet. Either way, you should have an appointment arranged for your pup before you pick him up and plan on taking him for an examination before bringing him home.

 The pup's first visit will consist of an overall examination to make sure that the pup does not have any problems that are not apparent to the eye. The veterinary surgeon will also set up a schedule for the pup's vaccina-

DID YOU KNOW?

Thoroughly puppy-proof your house before bringing your puppy home. Never use roach or rodent poisons in any area accessible to the puppy. Avoid the use of toilet bowl cleaners. Most dogs are born with toilet bowl sonar and will take a drink if the lid is left open. Also keep the trash secured and out of reach.

53

tions; the breeder will inform you of which ones the pup has already received and the vet can continue from there.

Make your Westie feel welcome to your home, but don't overwhelm him in the first day. He's already had a long, rough day!

INTRODUCTION TO THE FAMILY

Everyone in the house will be excited about the puppy coming home and will want to pet him and play with him, but it is best to make the introduction low-key so as not to overwhelm the puppy. He is apprehensive already. It is the first time he has been separated from his mother and the breeder, and the ride to your home is likely the first time he has been in an auto. The last thing you want to do is smother him, as this will only frighten him further. This is not to say that human contact is not extremely necessary at this stage, because this is the time when a connection between the pup and

his human family is formed. Gentle petting and soothing words should help console him, as well as just putting him down and letting him explore on his own (under your watchful eye, of course).

The pup may approach the family members or may busy himself with exploring for a while. Gradually, each person should spend some time with the pup, one at a time, crouching down to get as close to the pup's level as possible and letting him sniff their hands and petting him gently. He definitely needs human attention and he needs to be touched—this is how to form an immediate bond. Just remember that the pup is experiencing a lot of things for the first time, at the same time. There are new people, new noises, new smells, and new things to investigate: so be gentle, be affectionate, and be as comforting as you can.

DID YOU KNOW?

Scour your carport for potential puppy dangers. Remove weed killers, pesticides and antifreeze materials. Antifreeze is highly toxic and even a few drops can kill an adult dog. The sweet taste attracts the animal, who will quickly consume it from the floor or curbside.

YOUR PUP'S FIRST NIGHT HOME

You have travelled home with your new charge safely in his basket or crate. He's been to the vet for a thorough check-over; he's keep in mind that this is puppy's first night ever to be sleeping alone. His dam and littermates are no longer at paw's length and he's a bit scared, cold and lonely. Be reassuring to your new family

Your new Westie puppy must be under constant supervision. He might find himself in a dangerous situation, especially if he tries to explore the garden by himself.

been weighed, his papers examined; perhaps he's even been vaccinated and wormed as well. He's met the family, licked the whole family, including the excited children and the less-than-happy cat. He's explored his area, his new bed, the garden and anywhere else he's been permitted. He's eaten his first meal at home and relieved himself in the proper place. He's heard lots of new sounds, smelled new friends and seen more of the outside world than ever before.

That was just the first day! He's tuckered out and is ready for bed…or so you think!

It's puppy's first night and you are ready to say 'Good night'—

member. This is not the time to spoil him and give in to his inevitable whining.

Puppies whine. They whine to let the others know where they are and hopefully to get company out of it. Place your pup in his new bed or crate in his room and close the door. Mercifully, he may fall asleep without a peep. If the inevitable occurs, ignore the whining: he is fine. Be strong and keep his interest in mind. Do not allow your heart to become guilty and visit the pup. He will fall asleep.

Many breeders recommend placing a piece of bedding from his former homestead in his new bed so that he recognises the scent of his littermates. Others still advise placing a hot water bottle in his bed for warmth. The latter may be a good idea provided the pup doesn't attempt to suckle—he'll get good and wet and may not fall asleep so fast.

Puppy's first night can be somewhat stressful for the pup and his new family. Remember that you are setting the tone of nighttime at your house. Unless you want to play with your pup every evening at 10 p.m., midnight and 2 a.m., don't initiate the habit. Your family will thank you, and so will your pup!

PREVENT PUPPY PROBLEMS
SOCIALISATION
Now that you have done all of the preparatory work and have helped your pup get accustomed to his new home and family, it is about time for you to have some fun! Socialising your West Highland White Terrier pup gives you the opportunity to show off your new friend, and your pup gets to reap the benefits of being an adorable furry creature that people want to pet and, in general, think is absolutely precious!

Besides getting to know his new family, your puppy should be exposed to other people, animals and situations. This will help him become well adjusted as he grows up and less prone to being timid or fearful of the new things he will encounter. Your pup's socialisation began at the breeder's but now it is your responsibility to continue it. The socialisation he receives up until the age of 12 weeks is the most critical, as this is the time when he forms his impressions of the outside world. Be especially careful during the eight-to-ten-week period, also known as the fear period. The interaction he receives during this time should be gentle and reassuring. Lack of socialisation can manifest itself in fear and aggression as the dog grows up. He needs lots of human contact, affection, handling and exposure to other animals.

Once your pup has received his necessary vaccinations, feel free to take him out and about (on his lead, of course). Walk him

DID YOU KNOW?
Thorough socialisation includes not only meeting new people but also being introduced to new experiences such as riding in the car, having his coat brushed, hearing the television, walking in a crowd—the list is endless. The more your pup experiences, and the more positive the experiences are, the less of a shock and the less scary it will be for your pup to encounter new things.

around the neighbourhood, take him on your daily errands, let people pet him, let him meet other dogs and pets, etc. Puppies do not have to try to make friends; there will be no shortage of people who will want to introduce themselves. Just make sure that you carefully supervise each meeting. If the neighbourhood children want to say hello, for example, that is great—children and pups most often make great companions. Sometimes an excited child can unintentionally handle a pup too roughly, or an overzealous pup can playfully nip a little too hard. You want to make socialisation experiences positive ones. What a pup learns during this very formative stage will impact his attitude toward future encounters. You want your dog to be comfortable around everyone. A pup that has a bad experience with a child may grow up to be a dog that is shy around or aggressive toward children.

Socialisation is important. Your new Westie should meet his human friends as well as his canine associates.

DID YOU KNOW?

It will take at least two weeks for your puppy to become accustomed to his new surroundings. Give him lots of love, attention, handling, frequent opportunities to relieve himself, a diet he likes to eat and a place he can call his own.

CONSISTENCY IN TRAINING

Dogs, being pack animals, naturally need a leader, or else they try to establish dominance in their packs. When you bring a dog into your family, the choice of who becomes the leader and who becomes the 'pack' is entirely up to you! Your pup's intuitive quest for dominance, coupled with the fact that it is nearly impossible to look at an adorable West Highland White Terrier pup, with his 'puppy-dog' eyes and his too-big-for-his-head ears, and not cave in, give the pup almost an unfair advantage in getting the upper hand! A pup will definitely test the waters to see what he can and cannot do. Do not give in to those pleading eyes—stand your ground when it comes to disciplining the pup and make sure that all family members do the same. It will only confuse the pup when Mother tells him to get off the couch when he is used to sitting up there with Father to watch the nightly news. Avoid discrepancies by having all members of the

Early training pays you dividends for the life of your dog. The Westie's personality is shaped by early training.

household decide on the rules before the pup even comes home…and be consistent in enforcing them! Early training shapes the dog's personality, so you cannot be unclear in what you expect.

COMMON PUPPY PROBLEMS

The best way to prevent puppy problems is to be proactive in stopping an undesirable behaviour as soon as it starts. The old saying 'You can't teach an old dog new tricks' does not necessarily hold

true, but it is true that it is much easier to discourage bad behaviour in a young developing pup than to wait until the pup's bad behaviour becomes the adult dog's bad habit. There are some problems that are especially prevalent in puppies as they develop.

NIPPING

As puppies start to teethe, they feel the need to sink their teeth into anything available…unfortunately that includes your fingers, arms, hair, and toes. You may find this behaviour cute for the first five seconds…until you feel just how sharp those puppy teeth are. This is something you want to discourage immediately and consistently with a firm 'No!' (or whatever number of firm 'No's' it takes for him to understand that you mean business). Then replace your finger with an appropriate chew toy. Whilst this behaviour is merely annoying when the dog is young, it can become dangerous as your West Highland White Terrier's adult teeth grow in and his jaws develop, and he continues to think it is okay to gnaw on human appendages. Your Westie does not mean any harm with a friendly nip, but he also does not know his own strength.

CRYING/WHINING

Your pup will often cry, whine, whimper, howl or make some type of commotion when he is left alone. This is basically his way of calling out for attention to make sure that you know he is there and that you have not forgotten about him. He feels insecure when he is left alone, when you are out of the house and he is in his crate or when you are in another part of the house and he cannot see you. The noise he is making is an expression of the anxiety he feels at being alone, so he needs to be taught that being alone is okay. You are not actually training the dog to stop making noise, you are training him to feel comfortable when he is alone and thus removing the need for him to make the noise. This is where the crate filled with cosy blankets comes in handy. You want to know that he is safe when you are not there to supervise, and you know that he will be safe in his crate rather than roaming freely about the house. In order for the pup to stay in his crate without making a fuss, he needs to be comfortable in his crate. On that note, it is extremely important that the crate is never used as a form of punishment, or the pup will have a negative association with the crate.

Accustom the pup to the crate in short, gradually increasing time intervals in which you put him in the crate, maybe with a treat, and stay in the room with him. If he cries or makes a fuss, do not go to him, but stay in his sight.

Gradually he will realise that staying in his crate is all right without your help, and it will not be so traumatic for him when you are not around. You may want to leave the radio on softly when you leave the house; the sound of human voices may be comforting to him.

DID YOU KNOW?

Chewing goes hand in hand with nipping in the sense that a teething puppy is always looking for a way to soothe his aching gums. In this case, instead of chewing on you, he may have taken a liking to your favourite shoe or something else which he should not be chewing. Again, realise that this is a normal canine behaviour that does not need to be discouraged, only redirected. Your pup just needs to be taught what is acceptable to chew on and what is off limits. Consistently tell him NO when you catch him chewing on something forbidden and give him a chew toy. Conversely, praise him when you catch him chewing on something appropriate. In this way you are discouraging the inappropriate behaviour and reinforcing the desired behaviour. The puppy chewing should stop after his adult teeth have come in, but an adult dog continues to chew for various reasons—perhaps because he is bored, to relieve tension or he just likes to chew. That is why it is important to redirect his chewing when he is still young.

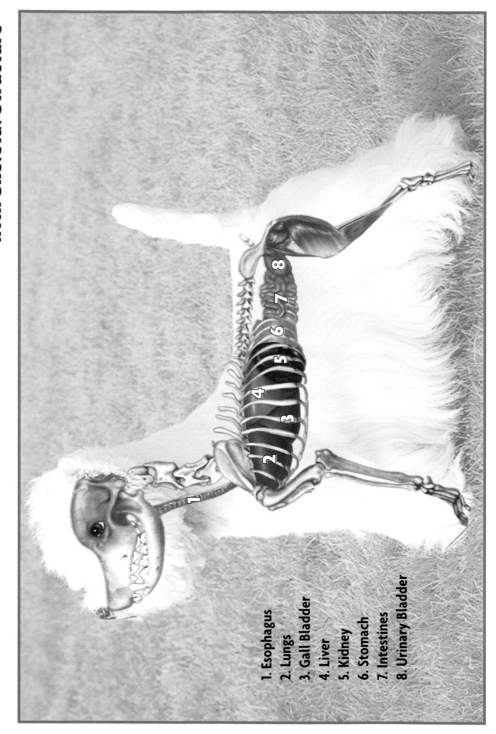

1. Esophagus
2. Lungs
3. Gall Bladder
4. Liver
5. Kidney
6. Stomach
7. Intestines
8. Urinary Bladder

DIETARY AND FEEDING CONSIDERATIONS

You have probably heard it a thousand times, 'you are what you eat.' Believe it or not, it's very true. Dogs are what you feed them because they have little choice in the matter. Even those people who truly want to feed their dogs the best often cannot do so because they do not know which foods are best for their dog.

Dog foods are produced in three basic types: dried, semi-moist and tinned. Dried foods are the choice of the cost conscious because they are much less expensive than semi-moist and canned. Dried foods contain the least fat and the most preserva-

DID YOU KNOW?
Selecting the best dried dog food is difficult. There is no majority consensus amongst veterinary scientists as to the value of nutrient analyses (protein, fat, fibre, moisture, ash, cholesterol, minerals, etc.). All agree that feeding trials are what matters, but you also have to consider the individual dog. Its weight, age, activity and what pleases its taste all must be considered. It is probably best to take the advice of your veterinary surgeon. Every dog's dietary requirements vary, even during the lifetime of a particular dog.

If your dog is fed a good dried food, it does not require supplements of meat or vegetables. Dogs do appreciate a little variety in their diets so you may choose to stay with the same brand, but vary the flavour. Alternatively you may wish to add a little flavoured stock to give a difference to the taste.

You cannot have a happy, healthy Westie if you offer him a poor diet. A balanced dog food and plenty of water are essential; follow the advice of your veterinary surgeon.

tives. Most tinned foods are 60–70-percent water, whilst semi-moist foods are so full of sugar that they are the least preferred by owners, though dogs welcome

Newborn puppies should begin suckling almost immediately. If they fail to suckle when placed onto their mother's teat, they must be hand fed on a special formula.

them (as a child does sweets).

Three stages of development must be considered when selecting a diet for your dog: the puppy stage, the mid-age or adult stage and the senior age or geriatric stage.

DID YOU KNOW?
Dog food must be at room temperature, neither too hot nor too cold. Fresh water, changed daily and served in a clean bowl, is mandatory, especially when feeding dried food.

Never feed your dog from the table while you are eating. Never feed your dog left-overs from your own meal. They usually contain too much fat and too much seasoning.

Dogs must chew their food. Hard pellets are excellent; soups and slurries are to be avoided.

Don't add left-overs or any extras to normal dog food. The normal food is usually balanced and adding something extra destroys the balance.

Except for age-related changes, dogs do not require dietary variations. They can be fed the same basic diet, day after day, without their becoming ill.

DID YOU KNOW?
A good test for proper diet is the colour, odour, and firmness of your dog's stool. A healthy dog usually produces three semi-hard stools per day. The stools should have no unpleasant odour. They should be the same colour from excretion to excretion.

PUPPY STAGE
Puppies have a natural instinct to suck milk from their mother's teats. They exhibit this behaviour from the first moments of their lives. If they don't suckle within a short while, the breeder attempts to put them onto their mother's nipple. A newborn's failure to suckle often requires that the breeder handfeed the pup under the guidance of a veterinary surgeon. This involves a baby bottle and a special formula. Their mother's milk is much better than any formula because it contains colostrum, a sort of antibiotic milk that protects the puppy during the first eight to ten weeks of their lives.

Puppies should be allowed to nurse for six weeks and they should be slowly weaned away from their mother by introducing small portions of tinned meat after they are about one month old. Dried food is then gradually added to the puppies' portions over the next few weeks.

By the time they are eight weeks old, they should be completely weaned and fed solely a puppy dry food. During this weaning period, their diet is most important as the puppy grows fastest during its first year of life.

West Highland White Terrier pups should be fed three meals per day when they are six to eight

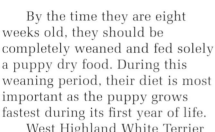

weeks of age. At eight weeks, the pup can be fed twice per day. Fussy eaters may require an additional smaller meal to maintain a good weight. Growth foods can be recommended by your veterinary surgeon and the puppy should be kept on this diet for up to 18 months.

Puppy diets should be balanced for your dog's needs,

At six weeks of age, puppies are introduced to tinned meat. Most Westie pups wean with no problems from the dam.

Cheers for tasty victuals! Westies are usually hearty eaters that do not need much encouragement at dinner time.

Food treats can be used as motivators in training or rewards for a job well done, but be careful not to give your Westie too many treats.

and supplements of vitamins, minerals and protein should not be necessary.

ADULT DIETS

A dog is considered an adult when it has stopped growing in height and/or length. Do not consider the dog's weight when the decision is made to switch from a puppy diet to a maintenance diet. Again you should rely upon your veterinary surgeon to recommend an acceptable maintenance diet. Major dog food manufacturers specialise in this type of food and it is just necessary for you to select the one best suited to your dog's needs. Active dogs may have different requirements than sedate dogs.

A West Highland White Terrier is fully mature around 12 months of age, though it often takes another 12 to 18 months for dog to reach its peak as a performance animal.

SENIOR DIETS

As dogs get older, their metabolism changes. The older dog usually exercises less, moves more slowly and sleeps more. This change in lifestyle and physiological performance requires a change in diet. Since these changes take place slowly, they might not be recognisable. What is easily recognisable is weight gain. By continually feeding your dog an adult mainte-

As your Westie grows, his nutritional needs will change. Your vet can help you plan a proper feeding schedule for your dog.

DID YOU KNOW?
You must store your dried dog food carefully. Open packages of dog food quickly lose their vitamin value, usually within 90 days of being opened. Mould spores and vermin could also contaminate the food.

nance diet when it is slowing down metabolically, your dog will gain weight. Obesity in an older dog compounds the health problems that already accompany old age.

As dogs get older, few of their organs function up to par. The kidneys slow down and the intestines become less efficient. These age-related factors are best handled with a change in diet and a change in feeding schedule to give smaller portions that are more easily digested.

There is no single best diet for every older dog. Whilst many dogs do well on light or senior diets, other dogs do better on

puppy diets or other special premium diets such as lamb and rice.

Be sensitive to your senior West Highland White Terrier's diet and this will help control other problems that may arise with your old friend.

Westies do not need organised trials to get proper exercise, but trained Westies thrive on the challenge and activity.

WATER

Just as your dog needs proper nutrition from his food, water is an essential 'nutrient' as well. Water keeps the dog's body properly hydrated and promotes normal function of the body's systems. During housebreaking it is necessary to keep an eye on how much water your West Highland White Terrier is drinking, but once he is reliably trained he should have access to clean fresh water at all times. Make sure that the dog's water bowl is clean, and change the water often.

EXERCISE

All dogs require some form of exercise, regardless of breed. A sedentary lifestyle is as harmful to a dog as it is to a person. The West Highland White Terrier happens to be an above-active breed that requires more exercise than most breeds. Regular walks, play sessions in the garden, or letting the dog run free in the garden under your supervision are

Some dogs can be a bit sloppy about their feeding and drinking habits. This large cat pan solved the messy floor problem easily.

DID YOU KNOW?

Many adult diets are based on grain. There is nothing wrong with this as long as it does not contain soy meal. Diets based on soy often cause flatulence (passing gas).

Grain-based diets are almost always the least expensive and a good grain diet is just as good as the most expensive diet containing animal protein.

There are many cases, however, when your dog might require a special diet. These special requirements should only be recommended by your veterinary surgeon.

65

Read the label on the dog food you are using. Many dog foods only report about half of the contents of the dog food. Become an educated dog owner.

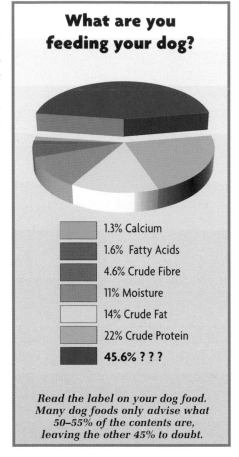

What are you feeding your dog?

- 1.3% Calcium
- 1.6% Fatty Acids
- 4.6% Crude Fibre
- 11% Moisture
- 14% Crude Fat
- 22% Crude Protein
- **45.6% ? ? ?**

Read the label on your dog food. Many dog foods only advise what 50–55% of the contents are, leaving the other 45% to doubt.

in some type of destructive behaviour. In this sense, it is essential for the owner's mental well being as well!

GROOMING
Do understand before purchasing your Westie that this is a breed with a coat that needs maintenance, whether you have a dog for the show ring or one that is a household pet. Think of it in terms of your child—you bathe your youngster, comb his hair and put a clean set of clothes on him. The end product is that you have a child who smells good, looks nice, and whom you enjoy having in your company. It is the same with your dog —keep the dog brushed, cleaned and trimmed

all sufficient forms of exercise for the West Highland White Terrier. For those who are more ambitious, you will find that your West Highland White Terrier will be able to keep up with you on extra long walks or the morning run. Not only is exercise essential to keep the dog's body fit, it is essential to his mental well being. A bored dog will find something to do, which often manifests itself

DID YOU KNOW?
Holland Buckley wrote in 1913: 'Most people wash their dogs regularly. Unless preparing a puppy for a special purpose, do not bathe him at all, at least not artificially, but get him used to swimming in a pond or the river, never forgetting to give him a good gallop and a rub down afterwards. A few minutes spent each day with a comb and a dandy brush will keep the coat in tip-top condition, and the skin supple and healthy.'

and you will find it a pleasure to be in his company. However, it will require some effort to do this.

The Westie is a double-coated dog. There is a dense, thick undercoat that protects the dog in all kinds of weather and there is a harsh outercoat. Coat care for the pet Westie can be much different and easier than the coat care for a show dog. The vast majority of Westie fanciers have pet dogs and they should not expect to maintain show coats.

If you are planning to show your West Highland White Terrier, you will be ahead of the game if you purchase your puppy from a reputable breeder who grooms and shows her dogs. If so, this is the individual to see for grooming lessons to learn how to get your dog ready for the show ring. Grooming for show is an art, and an art that cannot be learned in a few months. Furthermore, it is very difficult—but not impossi-

ble—to learn it from a book.

The primary difference between the pet and show Westie coat is that the show Westie will have a dense undercoat and on top of it he will have a shiny, harsh coat that will fit him like a jacket. With the proper coat, the dog presents a smartness in the ring that can be hard to beat. This coat can only be acquired by stripping the body coat with a stripping knife or stripping by hand. Within 10 to 12 weeks, and with the proper upkeep, he will have grown from his 'underwear' outfit stage into a smart new outfit

Whether pet dog or show dog, all Westies need regular grooming for healthy coats and skin.

Westies are great showmen. The Westie show coat is more dramatic than the pet clip, requiring many hours of stripping and preening.

67

A pin brush is used to groom the top of the head.

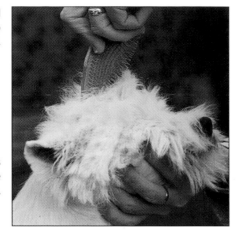

Grooming tools needed for the show Westie.

Chalk is used to 'whiten' the Westie's coat. Professionals never get caught with dust on them!

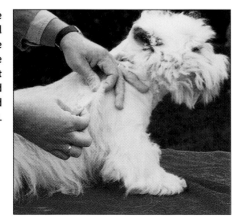

Westies require professional grooming for the show ring. The Westie show coat is plucked by hand to get the desired rough appearance.

ready for the ring. This all takes skill, time and interest in order to do it well.

Pet grooming is different from grooming for the show ring as you use a clipper on the body and scissors for trimming the furnishings. You will not have the harsh,

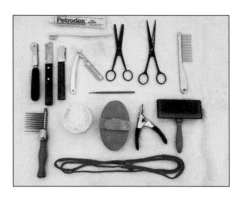

tight-fitting jacket of the show Westie, but you will have a neat, clean and trimmed dog that will still look like a West Highland White Terrier. Even those with kennels who are active in the show ring will clip their old dogs or those who are no longer being shown.

Here are the tools that you will need if you are going to do your own grooming:

1. A grooming table, something sturdy with a rubber mat covering the top. You will need a grooming arm, or a 'hanger.' (You can use a table in your laundry room with an eye hook in the ceiling for holding the leash.) Your dog will now be

comfortable even if confined and you will be able to work on the dog. Grooming is a very difficult and frustrating job if you try to groom without a table and a grooming arm.

2. A metal comb, a slicker brush, a good, sharp pair of scissors and a toenail trimmer.

3. Electric clippers with a #10 blade.

To start: Set your dog on the table and put the leash around his neck. Have your leash up behind the ears and have the leash taut when you fasten it to your eye hook. Do not walk away and leave your dog unattended as he can jump off the table and be left dangling from the leash with his feet scrambling around in the air.

Take your slicker brush and

A scissors is used to trim the anal region to keep it tidy.

A metal comb is used to groom the trunk.

The hair on the chest may be tidied with scissors.

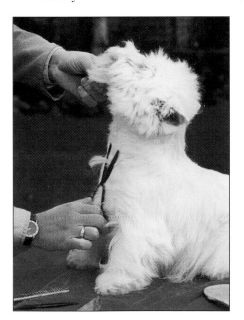

brush out the entire coat. Brush the whiskers toward the nose, the body hair toward the tail, the tail up toward the tip of the tail. Brush the leg furnishings up toward the body and brush the chest hair down toward the table. Hold the dog up by the front legs and gently brush the stomach hair, first toward the head and then back toward the rear. For cleanliness, you may want to take your scissors and trim the area around the penis. With the girls,

69

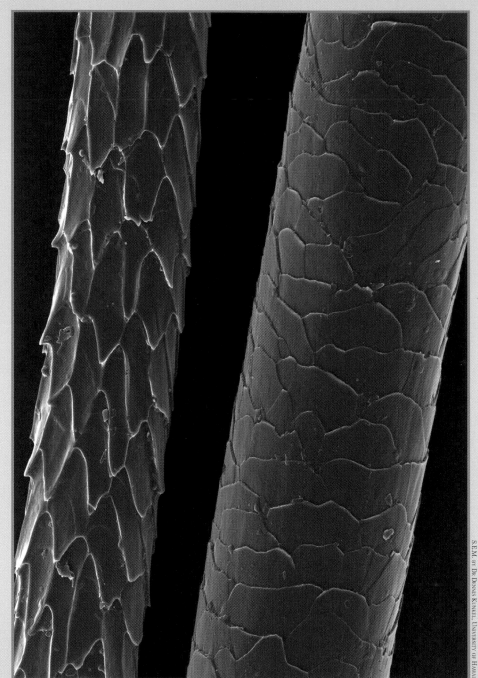

A highly magnified top coat and undercoat hair sample from a healthy West Highland White Terrier. The thick hair is coarse with a heavy cuticle (outer sheathing). The fine hair is soft with a completely different cuticle when compared with the outer coat.

S.E.M. BY DR DENNIS KUNKEL, UNIVERSITY OF HAWAII

trim some of the hair around the vulva.

Now that your dog is brushed out, comb through the coat with your metal comb. By now you have removed a fair amount of dead hair and your dog will already be looking better. You may find some small matts and these can be worked out with your fingers or your comb. If you brush your dog out every week or so, you will not have too much of a problem with the matts.

We are now at the stage where you will take your clippers in hand. Your dog will only need to be clipped every three months or so, but you may want to touch up the head more often. Start with the head and follow this pattern:

Take your clippers and clip the neck, shoulders, and body. Be sure to trim in the direction that the hair lies. Now, take your comb and comb the leg hair down toward the table.

Take your scissors and trim the legs neatly. You can also trim off anything that 'sticks out.' If this is your first experience, you may be a bit clumsy, but the hair will grow back in a short time. The finished product may not be quite what you had expected, but expertise will come with experience and you will soon be very proud of your efforts. Your dog should now look like a West Highland White Terrier.

Put your dog in the laundry tub when you are finished and give him a good bath and rinsing. After towelling him down, return

Purchase a toothpaste made for dogs and brush your Westie's teeth at least once a week. This does wonders for his teeth and his breath!

him to the grooming table and trim the toenails on all four legs. At this point you can dry your dog with a blaster and brush him out again. Or, you can let him dry naturally and then brush him out.

71

Dry your Westie as thoroughly as possible before you remove him from the tub. Once he is placed on the floor, stand back, as he is destined to shake vigorously to rid the water from his coat.

DID YOU KNOW?

The use of human soap products like shampoo, bubble bath and hand soap can be damaging to a dog's coat and skin. Human products are too strong and remove the protective oils coating the dog's hair and skin (making him water-resistant). Use only shampoo made especially for dogs and you may like to use a medicated shampoo which will always help to keep external parasites at bay.

DID YOU KNOW?

Once you are sure that the dog is thoroughly rinsed, squeeze the excess water out of the coat with your hand and dry him with a heavy towel. You may choose to use a blaster on his coat or just let it dry naturally. In cold weather, never allow your dog outside with a wet coat.

There are 'dry bath' products on the market, which are sprays and powders intended for spot cleaning, that can be used between regular baths, if necessary. They are not substitutes for regular baths, but they are easy to use for touch-ups as they do not require rinsing.

If you have grooming problems, you can take your dog to the professional groomer the first time or two for his grooming. The groomer will 'set' the pattern and then it will be easier for you to get the Westie look by following the pattern that is already set in the coat. (Of course, you can eliminate all of the grooming for yourself, except for the weekly brushing, if you take your dog to the groomer every three months!) If the coat totally grows out before you start to groom, the pattern will be lost and then you will have to start over again. Just remember, many pet owners can do a much better job trimming their dogs than some professional groomers.

To wrap it up: Your pet should be brushed weekly and bathed as needed. Trim the

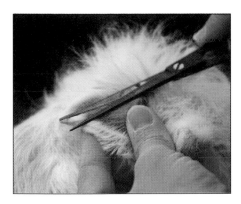

Excess hairs inside the ears should be carefully trimmed with scissors.

toenails every month or so and plan to clip the dog every three months. Follow this plan and your dog will be clean, he will have a new dress every three months, and he will look like a West Highland White Terrier!

EAR CLEANING

The ears should be kept clean and any excess hair inside the ear should be trimmed. Ears can be cleaned with a cotton wipe and special cleaner or ear powder made especially for dogs. Be on the lookout for any signs of infection or ear mite infestation. If

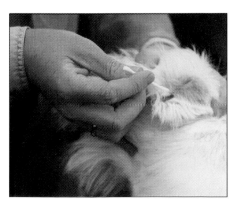

your West Highland White Terrier has been shaking his head or scratching at his ears frequently, this usually indicates a problem. If his ears have an unusual odour, this is a sure sign of mite infestation or infection, and a signal to have his ears checked by the veterinary surgeon.

NAIL CLIPPING

Your West Highland White Terrier should be accustomed to having his nails trimmed at an early age,

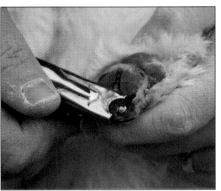

The nails are cut with a special dog nail clipper.

since it will be part of your maintenance routine throughout his life. Not only does it look nicer, but a dog with long nails can cause injury if he jumps up or if he scratches someone unintentionally. Also, a long nail has a better chance of ripping and bleeding, or causing the feet to spread. A good rule of thumb is that if you can hear your dog's nails clicking on the floor when he walks, his nails are too long.

Clean the ears with a cotton wipe or swab. Be very careful not to enter the canal of the ear.

Before you start cutting, make sure you can identify the 'quick' in each nail. The quick is a blood vessel that runs through the centre of each nail and grows rather close to the end. It will bleed if accidentally cut, which will be quite painful for the dog as it contains nerve endings. Keep some type of clotting agent on hand, such as a styptic pencil or styptic powder (the type used for shaving). This will stop the bleeding quickly when applied to the end of the cut nail. Do not panic if this happens, just stop the bleeding and talk soothingly to

DID YOU KNOW?

A dog that spends a lot of time outside on a hard surface such as cement or pavement will have his nails naturally worn down and may not need to have them trimmed as often, except maybe in the colder months when he is not outside as much. Regardless, it is best to get your dog accustomed to this procedure at an early age so that he is used to it. Some dogs are especially sensitive about having their feet touched, but if a dog has experienced it since he was young, he should not be bothered by it.

Never cut through the quick. Only remove the very tip of the nail. Be especially careful with black nails.

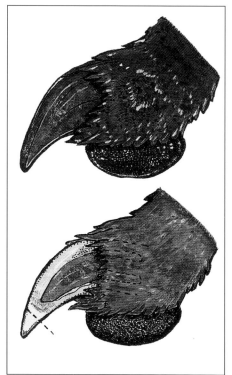

your dog. Once he has calmed down, move on to the next nail. It is better to clip a little at a time, particularly with black-nailed dogs.

Hold your pup steady as you begin trimming his nails; you do not want him to make any sudden movements or run away. Talk to him soothingly and stroke his fur as you clip. Holding his foot in your hand, simply take off the end of each nail in one quick clip. You can purchase nail clippers that are specially made for dogs; you can probably find them wherever you buy pet or grooming supplies.

TRAVELLING WITH YOUR DOG
CAR TRAVEL
You should accustom your West Highland White Terrier to riding

Whether travelling across town or across country, the proper way to transport any dog is in a crate in the rear of the vehicle.

The crate is the safest way to travel by car with your Westie. Travelling unrestrained in a car with open windows can be potentially dangerous.

hold him on his lap whilst you drive. Another option is a special-ly made safety harness for dogs, which straps the dog in much like a seat belt. Do not let the dog roam loose in the vehicle—this is very dangerous! If you should stop short, your dog can be thrown and injured. If the dog starts climbing on you and pester-ing you whilst you are driving, you will not be able to concen-trate on the road. It is an unsafe situation for everyone—human and canine.

For long trips, be prepared to stop to let the dog relieve himself. Bring along whatever you need to

in a car at an early age. You may or may not take him in the car often, but at the very least he will need to go to the vet and you do not want these trips to be traumat-ic for the dog or a big hassle for you. The safest way for a dog to ride in the car is in his crate. If he uses a fibreglass crate in the house, you can use the same crate for travel. Wire crates can be used for travel, but fibreglass or wooden crates are safer.

Put the pup in the crate and see how he reacts. If he seems uneasy, you can have a passenger

clean up after him. You should bring along some old towels and rags, should he have an accident in the car or become carsick.

AIR TRAVEL

If bringing your dog on a flight, you will have to contact the airline to make special arrangements. In Britain it is rather uncommon for dogs to travel by air, so advance permission is always required. The dog will be required to travel in a fibreglass crate; you may be able to use your own or the airline can supply one. To help the dog be at ease, put one of his favourite toys in the crate with him. Do not feed the dog for at least six hours before the trip to minimise his need to relieve himself. However, certain regulations specify that water

DID YOU KNOW?

For international travel you will have to make arrangements well in advance (perhaps months), as countries' regulations pertaining to bringing in animals differ. There may be special health certificates and/or vaccinations that your dog will need before taking the trip, sometimes this has to be done within a certain time frame. In rabies-free countries, you will need to bring proof of the dog's rabies vaccination and there may be a quarantine period upon arrival.

DID YOU KNOW?

If you are going on a long car trip with your dog, be sure the hotels are dog friendly. Many hotels do not accept dogs. Also take along some ice that can be thawed and offered to your dog if he becomes overheated. Most dogs like to lick ice.

must always be made available to the dog in the crate.

Make sure your dog is properly identified and that your contact information appears on his ID tags and on his crate. Animals travel in a different area of the plane than human passengers, and, although transporting animals is fairly routine for certain airlines, there is always the slight risk of getting separated from your dog.

BOARDING

So you want to take a family holiday—and you want to include all members of the family. You would probably make arrangements for accommodations ahead of time anyway, but this is especially important when travelling with a dog. You do not want to make an overnight stop at the only place around for miles and find out that they do not allow dogs. Also, you do not want to reserve a place for your family without confirming that you are

choose to board him at a kennel, you should stop by to see the facility and where the dogs are kept to make sure that it is clean. Talk to some of the employees and see how they treat the dogs— do they spend time with the dogs, play with them, exercise them, etc.? You know that your West

Your Westie will probably be much happier and safer in a proper dog kennel than travelling with you on a long trip.

travelling with a dog because if it is against their policy you may not have a place to stay.

Alternatively, if you are travelling and choose not to bring your West Highland White Terrier, you will have to make arrangements for him whilst you are away. Some options are to bring him to a neighbour's house to stay whilst you are gone, to have a trusted neighbour stop by often or stay at your house, or bring your dog to a reputable boarding kennel. If you

DID YOU KNOW?

If your dog gets lost, he is not able to ask for directions home.

Identification tags fastened to the collar give important information—the dog's name, the owner's name, the owner's address and a telephone number where the owner can be reached. This makes it easy for whoever finds the dog to contact the owner and arrange to have the dog returned. An added advantage is

DID YOU KNOW?

When travelling, never let your dog off-lead in a strange area. Your dog could run away out of fear or decide to chase a passing chipmunk or cat or simply want to stretch his legs without restriction—you might never see your canine friend again.

that a person will be more likely to approach a lost dog who has ID tags on his collar; it tells the person that this is somebody's pet rather than a stray. This is the easiest and fastest method of identification provided that the tags stay on the collar and the collar stays on the dog.

DID YOU KNOW?
You have a valuable dog. If the dog is lost or stolen you would undoubtedly become extremely upset. If you encounter a lost dog, notify the police or the local animal shelter.

DID YOU KNOW?
As puppies become more and more expensive, especially those puppies of high quality for showing and/or breeding, they have a greater chance of being stolen. The usual collar dog tag is, of course, easily removed. But there are two techniques that have become widely utilised for identification.

The puppy microchip implantation involves the injection of a small microchip, about the size of a corn kernel, under the skin of the dog. If your dog shows up at a clinic or shelter, or is offered for resale under less than savory circumstances, it can be positively identified by the microchip. The microchip is scanned and a registry quickly identifies you as the owner. This is not only protection against theft, but should the dog run away or go chasing a squirrel and get lost, you have a fair chance of getting it back.

Tattooing is done on various parts of the dog, from its belly to its cheeks. The number tattooed can be your telephone number or any other number which you can easily memorise. When professional dog thieves see a tattooed dog, they usually lose interest in it. Both microchipping and tattooing can be done at your local veterinary clinic. For the safety of our dogs, no laboratory facility or dog broker will accept a tattooed dog as stock.

Highland White Terrier will not be happy unless he gets regular activity. Also find out the kennel's policy on vaccinations and what they require. This is for all of the dogs' safety, since when dogs are kept together there is a greater risk of diseases being passed from dog to dog.

IDENTIFICATION
Your West Highland White Terrier is your valued companion and friend. That is why you always keep a close eye on him and you have made sure that he cannot escape from the garden or wriggle out of his collar and run away from you. However, accidents can happen and there may come a time when your dog unexpectedly gets separated from you. If this unfortunate event should occur, the first thing on your mind will be finding him. Proper identification, including an ID tag, a tattoo, and possibly a microchip, will increase the chances of his being returned to you safely and quickly.

POISONOUS PLANTS

Below is a partial list of plants that are considered poisonous. These plants can cause skin irritation, illness, and even death. You should be aware of the types of plants that grow in your garden and that you keep in your home. Special care should be taken to rid your garden of dangerous plants and to keep all plants in the household out of your West Highland White Terrier's reach.

American Blue Flag	Japanese Yew
Bachelor's Button	Jerusalem Cherry
Barberry	Jimson Weed
Bog Iris	Lenten Rose
Boxwood	Lily of the Valley
Buttercup	Marigold
Cherry Pits	Milkwort
Chinese Arbor	Mistletoe (berries)
Chokecherry	Monkshood
Christmas Rose	Mullein
Climbing Lily	Narcissus
Crown of Thorns	Peony
Elderberry (berries)	Persian Ivy
Elephant Ear	Rhododendron
English Ivy	Rhubarb
False Acacia	Shallon
Fern	Siberian Iris
Foxglove	Solomon's Seal
Hellebore	Star of Bethlehem
Herb of Grace	Water Lily
Holly	Wood Spurge
Horse Chestnut	Wisteria
Iris (bulb)	Yew

Canine Development Schedule

It is important to understand how and at what age a puppy develops into adulthood. If you are a puppy owner, consult the following Canine Development Schedule to determine the stage of development your West Highland White Terrier puppy is currently experiencing. This knowledge will help you as you work with the puppy in the weeks and months ahead.

Period	Age	Characteristics
FIRST TO THIRD	BIRTH TO SEVEN WEEKS	Puppy needs food, sleep and warmth, and responds to simple and gentle touching. Needs mother for security and disciplining. Needs littermates for learning and interacting with other dogs. Pup learns to function within a pack and learns pack order of dominance. Begin socialising with adults and children for short periods. Begins to become aware of its environment.
FOURTH	EIGHT TO TWELVE WEEKS	Brain is fully developed. Needs socialising with outside world. Remove from mother and littermates. Needs to change from canine pack to human pack. Human dominance necessary. Fear period occurs between 8 and 16 weeks. Avoid fright and pain.
FIFTH	THIRTEEN TO SIXTEEN WEEKS	Training and formal obedience should begin. Less association with other dogs, more with people, places, situations. Period will pass easily if you remember this is pup's change-to-adolescence time. Be firm and fair. Flight instinct prominent. Permissiveness and over-disciplining can do permanent damage. Praise for good behaviour.
JUVENILE	FOUR TO EIGHT MONTHS	Another fear period about 7 to 8 months of age. It passes quickly, but be cautious of fright and pain. Sexual maturity reached. Dominant traits established. Dog should understand sit, down, come and stay by now.

NOTE: THESE ARE APPROXIMATE TIME FRAMES. ALLOW FOR INDIVIDUAL DIFFERENCES IN PUPPIES.

West Highland White Terrier

Living with an untrained dog is a lot like owning a piano that you do not know how to play—it is a nice object to look at but it does not do much more than that to bring you pleasure. Now try taking piano lessons and suddenly the piano comes alive and brings forth magical sounds and rhythms that set your heart singing and your body swaying.

The same is true with your West Highland White Terrier. At first you enjoy seeing him around the house. He does not do much with you other than to need food, water and exercise. Come to think of it, he does not bring you much joy, either. He is a big responsibility with a very small return. Often

he develops unacceptable behaviours that annoy and/or infuriate you to say nothing of bad habits that may end up costing you great sums of money. Not a good thing!

Now train your West Highland White Terrier. Enrol in an

Well trained Westies that respect your wishes and obey your commands are a joy for their entire lifetimes. Westies are very intelligent and extremely trainable.

obedience class. Teach him good manners as you learn how and why he behaves the way he does. Find out how to communicate with your dog and how to recognise and understand his communications with you. Suddenly the dog takes on a new role in your life—he is smart, interesting, well behaved and fun to be with. He demonstrates his bond of devotion to you daily. In other words, your Westie does wonders for your ego because he

DID YOU KNOW?

If you start with a normal, healthy dog and give him time, patience and some carefully executed lessons, you will reap the rewards of that training for the life of the dog. And what a life it will be! The two of you will find immeasurable pleasure in the companionship you have built together with love, respect and understanding. Good luck and enjoy!

constantly reminds you that you are not only his leader, you are his hero! Miraculous things have happened—you have a wonderful dog (even your family and friends have noticed the transformation!) and you feel good about yourself.

Those involved with teaching dog obedience and counselling owners about their dogs' behaviour have discovered some interesting facts about dog

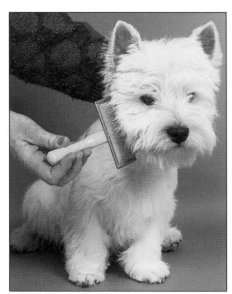

Grooming and training your Wesie go hand in hand. Accepting limits and discipline helps to mould the Westie into an obedient, pliable companion.

> **DID YOU KNOW?**
> Taking your dog to an obedience school may be the best investment in time and money you can ever make. You will enjoy the benefits for the lifetime of your dog and you will have the opportunity to meet people with similar expectations for their companion dogs.

capability and is willing to work patiently to help the dog succeed at developing to his fullest potential. Unfortunately, many owners of untrained adult dogs lack the patience factor, so they do not persist until their dogs are successful at learning particular behaviours.

Training a puppy aged 8 to 16 weeks (20 weeks at the most) is

ownership. For example, training dogs when they are puppies results in the highest rate of success in developing well-mannered and well-adjusted adult dogs. Training an older dog, from six months to six years of age, can produce almost equal results providing that the owner accepts the dog's slower rate of learning

> **DID YOU KNOW?**
> Dogs are the most honourable animals in existence. They consider another species (humans) as their own. They interface with you. You are their leader. Puppies perceive children to be on their level: their actions around small children are different than their behaviour around their adult masters.

like working with a dry sponge in a pool of water. The pup soaks up whatever you show him and constantly looks for more things to do and learn. At this early age, his body is not yet producing hormones, and therein lies the reason for such a high rate of success. Without hormones, he is focused on his owners and not particularly interested in investigating other places, dogs, people, etc. You are his leader: his

As the puppy gets older, it becomes more mature and, if not properly trained, can become unruly and even disrespectful.

DID YOU KNOW?
Dogs are as different from each other as people are. What works for one dog may not work for another. Have an open mind. If one method of training is unsuccessful, try another.

provider of food, water, shelter and security. He latches onto you and wants to stay close. He will usually follow you from room to room, will not let you out of his sight when you are outdoors with him, and respond in like manner to the people and animals you encounter. If you greet a friend warmly, he will be happy to greet the person as well. If, however, you are hesitant, even anxious, about the approach of a stranger, he will respond accordingly.

Once the puppy begins to produce hormones, his natural curiosity emerges and he begins to investigate the world around him. It is at this time when you may notice that the untrained dog begins to wander away from you

DID YOU KNOW?
Never train your dog, puppy or adult, when you are mad or in a sour mood. Dogs are very sensitive to human feelings, especially anger, and if your dog senses that you are angry or upset, he will connect your anger with his training and learn to resent or fear his training sessions.

and even ignore your commands to stay close. When this behaviour becomes a problem, the owner has two choices: get rid of the dog or train him. It is strongly urged that you choose the latter option.

Occasionally there are no classes available within a reasonable distance from the owner's home. Sometimes there are classes available but the tuition is too costly. Whatever the circumstances, the solution to the

You certainly want to train your Westie to relieve himself outside...but did you really want him to use your flower bed?

DID YOU KNOW?
If you want to be successful in training your dog, you have four rules to obey yourself:
1. Develop an understanding of how a dog thinks.
2. Do not blame the dog for lack of communication.
3. Define your dog's personality and act accordingly.
4. Have patience and be consistent.

DID YOU KNOW?
Stand up straight and authoritatively when giving your dog commands. Do not issue commands when lying on the floor or lying on your back on the sofa. If you are on your hands and knees when you give a command, your dog will think you are positioning yourself to play.

problem of lack of lesson availability lies within the pages of this book.

This chapter is devoted to helping you train your West Highland White Terrier at home. If the recommended procedures are followed faithfully, you may expect positive results that will prove rewarding to both you and your dog.

Whether your new charge is a puppy or a mature adult, the methods of teaching and the techniques we use in training basic behaviours are the same. After all, no dog, whether puppy or adult, likes harsh or inhumane methods. All creatures, however, respond favourably to gentle motivational methods and sincere praise and encouragement. Now let us get started.

HOUSEBREAKING
You can train a puppy to relieve itself wherever you choose. For example, city dwellers often train

their puppies to relieve themselves in the gutter because large plots of grass are not readily available. Suburbanites, on the other hand, usually have gardens to accommodate their dogs' needs.

Outdoor training includes such surfaces as grass, dirt and cement. Indoor training usually means training your dog to newspaper.

When deciding on the surface and location that you will want your West Highland White Terrier to use, be sure it is going to be permanent. Training your dog to grass and then changing your mind two months later is extremely difficult for both dog and owner.

Next, choose the command you will use each and every time you want your puppy to void. 'Go hurry up' and 'Go make' are examples of commands commonly used by dog owners.

'Is it time to go out yet?' This Westie wants to be let out so he can relieve himself. Don't test your Westie's body control by leaving him alone for hours on end.

Get in the habit of asking the puppy, 'Do you want to go hurry up?' (or whatever your chosen relief command is) before you take him out. That way, when he becomes an adult, you will be able to determine if he wants to

DID YOU KNOW?

Do not carry your dog to his toilet area. Lead him there on a leash or, better yet, encourage him to follow you to the spot. If you start carrying him to his spot, you might end up doing this routine forever and your dog will have the satisfaction of having trained YOU.

HOW MANY TIMES A DAY?

AGE	RELIEF TRIPS
To 14 weeks	10
14–22 weeks	8
22–32 weeks	6
Adulthood	4
(dog stops growing)	

These are estimates, of course, but they are a guide to the MINIMUM opportunities a dog should have each day to relieve itself.

An 8- to 12-week-old puppy will need to be taken outside frequently. Never let a puppy outside without proper supervision.

DID YOU KNOW?

Never line your pup's sleeping area with newspaper. Puppy litters are usually raised on newspaper and, once in your home, the puppy will immediately associate newspaper with voiding. Never put newspaper on any floor while housetraining, as this will only confuse the puppy. If you are paper-training him, use paper in his designated relief area ONLY. Finally, restrict water intake after evening meals. Offer a few licks at a time—never let a young puppy gulp water after meals.

go out when you ask him. A confirmation will be signs of interest, wagging his tail, watching you intently, going to the door, etc.

PUPPY'S NEEDS

Puppy needs to relieve himself after play periods, after each meal, after he has been sleeping and any time he indicates that he is looking for a place to urinate or defecate.

The urinary and intestinal tract muscles of very young puppies are not fully developed. Therefore, like human babies, puppies need to relieve themselves frequently.

Take your puppy out often—every hour for an eight-week-old, for example. The older the puppy, the less often he will need to relieve himself. Finally, as a mature healthy adult, he will require only three to five relief trips per day.

HOUSING

Since the types of housing and control you provide for your puppy have a direct relationship on the success of housetraining, we consider the various aspects of both before we begin training.

Bringing a new puppy home and turning him loose in your house can be compared to turning a child loose in a sports arena and telling the child that the place is all his! The sheer enormity of the place would be too much for him to handle.

Instead, offer the puppy clearly defined areas where he can play, sleep, eat and live. A room of the house where the family gathers is the most obvious choice. Puppies are social animals and need to feel a part of the pack right from the start. Hearing your voice, watching you whilst you are doing things and smelling you nearby are all positive reinforcers that he is now a member of your pack. Usually a family room, the kitchen or a nearby adjoining breakfast nook is ideal for providing safety and security for both puppy and owner.

Within that room there should be a smaller area which the puppy can call his own. A cubbyhole, a wire or fibreglass dog crate or a fenced (not boarded!) corner from which he can view the activities of his new family will be fine. The

Don't carry your Westie to his designated relief area. Let him walk there by himself on lead.

size of the area or crate is the key factor here. The area must be large enough for the puppy to lay down and stretch out as well as stand up without rubbing his head on the top, yet small enough so that he cannot relieve himself at one end and sleep at the other without

DID YOU KNOW?
Dogs will do anything for your attention. If you reward the dog when he is calm and resting, you will develop a well-mannered dog. If, on the other hand, you greet your dog excitedly and encourage him to wrestle and roughhouse with you, the dog will greet you the same way and you will have a hyper dog on your hands.

coming into contact with his droppings.

Dogs are, by nature, clean animals and will not remain close to their relief areas unless forced to do so. In those cases, they then become dirty dogs and usually remain that way for life.

The crate or cubby should be lined with a clean towel and offer one toy, no more. Do not put food or water in the crate, as eating and drinking will activate his digestive processes and ultimately defeat your purpose as well as make the puppy very uncomfortable as he attempts to 'hold it.'

CONTROL

By control, we mean helping the puppy to create a lifestyle pattern that will be compatible to that of his human pack (YOU!). Just as we guide little children to learn our way of life, we must show the puppy when it is time to play, eat, sleep, exercise and even entertain himself.

Your puppy should always sleep in his crate. He should also learn that, during times of household confusion and excessive human activity such as at breakfast when family members are preparing for the day, he can play by himself in relative safety and comfort in his crate. Each time you leave the puppy alone, he should be crated. Puppies are chewers. They cannot tell the difference between lamp cords, television wires, shoes, table legs, etc. Chewing into a television wire, for example, can be fatal to the puppy whilst a shorted wire can start a fire in the house.

If the puppy chews on the arm of the chair when he is alone, you will probably discipline him angrily when you get home. Thus, he makes the association that your coming home means he is going to be hit or punished. (He will not remember chewing up the chair and is incapable of making the association of the discipline with his naughty deed.)

Other times of excitement, such as family parties, etc., can be fun for the puppy providing he can view the activities from the security of his crate. He is not underfoot and he is not being fed

DID YOU KNOW?
The puppy should also have regular play and exercise sessions when he is with you or a family member. Exercise for a very young puppy can consist of a short walk around the house or garden. Playing can include fetching games with a large ball or a special raggy. (All puppies teethe and need soft things upon which to chew.) Remember to restrict play periods to indoors within his living area (the family room for example) until he is completely housetrained.

The exercise needs of a Westie include daily walks as well as a good jog about the garden.

all sorts of titbits that will probably cause him stomach distress, yet he still feels a part of the fun.

SCHEDULE

A puppy should be taken to his relief area each time he is released from his crate, after meals, after a play session, when he first awakens in the morning (at age eight weeks, this can mean 5 a.m.!). The puppy will indicate that he's ready 'to go' by circling or sniffing busily—do not misinterpret these signs. For a puppy less than ten weeks of age, a routine of taking him out every hour is necessary. As the puppy grows, he will be able to wait for longer periods of time.

Keep trips to his relief area short. Stay no more than five or six minutes and then return to the house. If he goes during that time, praise him lavishly and take him indoors immediately. If he does not, but he has an accident when you go back indoors, pick him up immediately, say 'No! No!' and return to his relief area. Wait a few minutes, then return to the house again. never hit a puppy or rub his face in urine or excrement when he has an accident!

Once indoors, put the puppy in his crate until you have had time to clean up his accident. Then release him to the family area and watch him more closely than before. Chances are, his accident was a result of your not picking up his signal or waiting too long before offering him the opportunity to relieve himself. Never hold a grudge against the puppy for accidents.

Let the puppy learn that going outdoors means it is time to relieve himself, not play. Once trained, he will be able to play indoors and out and still differentiate between the times for play versus the times for relief.

89

Help him develop regular hours for naps, being alone, playing by himself and just resting, all in his crate. Encourage him to entertain himself whilst you are busy with your activities. Let him learn that having you near is comforting, but it is not your main purpose in life to provide him with undivided attention.

Each time you put a puppy in his crate tell him, 'Crate time!' (or whatever command you choose). Soon, he will run to his crate when he hears you say those words.

In the beginning of his training, do not leave him in his crate for prolonged periods of time except during the night when everyone is sleeping. Make his experience with his crate a pleasant one and, as an adult, he will love his crate and willingly stay in it for several hours. There are millions of people who go to work every day and leave their adult dogs crated whilst they are away. The dogs accept this as their lifestyle and look forward to 'crate time.'

Crate training provides safety for you, the puppy and the home. It also provides the puppy with a feeling of security, and that helps the puppy achieve self-confidence and clean habits.

Remember that one of the primary ingredients in housetraining your puppy is control. Regardless of your lifestyle, there will always be occasions when you will need to have a place where your dog can stay and be happy and safe. Crate training is the answer for now and in the future.

In conclusion, a few key elements are really all you need for a successful house and crate training method—consistency, frequency, praise, control and supervision. By following these procedures with a normal, healthy puppy, you and the

DID YOU KNOW?

Practice Makes Perfect!

• Have training lessons with your dog every day in several short segments—three to five times a day for a few minutes at a time is ideal.

• Do not have long practice sessions. The dog will become easily bored.

• Never practice when you are tired, ill, worried or in an otherwise negative mood. This will transmit to the dog and may have an adverse effect on its performance.

Think fun, short and above all POSITIVE! End each session on a high note, rather than a failed exercise, and make sure to give a lot of praise. Enjoy the training and help your dog enjoy it, too.

THE SUCCESS METHOD
6 Steps to Successful Crate Training

1 Tell the puppy 'Crate time!' and place him in the crate with a small treat (a piece of cheese or half of a biscuit). Let him stay in the crate for five minutes while you are in the same room. Then release him and praise lavishly. Never release him when he is fussing. Wait until he is quiet before you let him out.

2 Repeat Step 1 several times a day.

3 The next day, place the puppy in the crate as before. Let him stay there for ten minutes. Do this several times.

4 Continue building time in five-minute increments until the puppy stays in his crate for 30 minutes with you in the room. Always take him to his relief area after prolonged periods in his crate.

5 Now go back to Step 1 and let the puppy stay in his crate for five minutes, this time while you are out of the room.

6 Once again, build crate time in five-minute increments with you out of the room. When the puppy will stay willingly in his crate (he may even fall asleep!) for 30 minutes with you out of the room, he will be ready to stay in it for several hours at a time.

DID YOU KNOW?

Most of all, be consistent. Always take your dog to the same location, always use the same command, and always have him on lead when he is in his relief area, unless a fenced-in garden is available.

By following the Success Method, your puppy will be completely housetrained by the time his muscle and brain development reach maturity. Keep in mind that small breeds usually mature faster than large breeds, but all puppies should be trained by six months of age.

Once your Westie is acclimated to his crate and completely housebroken, he will enjoy exploring both his designated area in the house and his time in the privacy of his crate.

puppy will soon be past the stage of 'accidents' and ready to move on to a full and rewarding life together.

ROLES OF DISCIPLINE, REWARD AND PUNISHMENT
Discipline, training one to act in accordance with rules, brings order to life. It is as simple as that. Without discipline, particularly in a group society, chaos reigns supreme and the group will

Rewards and praise are more effective in training than punishment. Although your Westie should behave to please you, an occasional bribe does wonders.

eventually perish. Humans and canines are social animals and need some form of discipline in order to function effectively. They must procure food, protect their home base and their young and reproduce to keep the species going.

Your Westie's identification tags should be securely attached to his collar at all times.

If there were no discipline in the lives of social animals, they would eventually die from starvation and/or predation by other stronger animals.

In the case of domestic canines, dogs need discipline in their lives in order to understand how their pack (you and other family members) functions and how they must act in order to survive.

A large humane society in a highly populated area recently surveyed dog owners regarding their satisfaction with their relationships with their dogs. People who had trained their dogs were 75% more satisfied with their pets than those who had never trained their dogs.

Dr Edward Thorndike, a psychologist, established *Thorndike's Theory of Learning*, which states that a behaviour that results in a pleasant event tends to be repeated. A behaviour that results in an unpleasant event tends not to be repeated. It is this theory on which training methods are based today. For example, if you manipulate a dog to perform a specific behaviour and reward him for doing it, he is likely to do it again because he enjoyed the end result.

Occasionally, punishment, a penalty inflicted for an offence, is

necessary. The best type of punishment often comes from an outside source. For example, a child is told not to touch the stove because he may get burned. He disobeys and touches the stove. In doing so, he receives a burn. From that time on, he respects the heat of the stove and avoids contact with it. Therefore, a behaviour that results in an unpleasant event tends not to be repeated.

A good example of a dog learning the hard way is the dog who chases the house cat. He is told many times to leave the cat alone, yet he persists in teasing the cat. Then, one day he begins chasing the cat but the cat turns and swipes a claw across the dog's face, leaving him with a painful gash on his nose. The final result is that the dog stops chasing the cat.

TRAINING EQUIPMENT
COLLAR

A simple buckle collar is fine for most dogs. One who pulls mightily on the leash may require a chain choker collar. Only in the most severe cases of a dog being totally out of control is the use of a prong or pinch collar recommended. These collars should only be used by owners with experience in the proper use of such equipment. In some areas, such as the United Kingdom, these types of collars are not allowed.

CHOOSE THE PROPER COLLAR

The buckle collar is the standard collar used for everyday purpose. Be sure that you adjust the buckle on growing puppies. Check it every day. It can become too tight overnight! These collars can be made of leather or nylon. Attach your dog's identification tags to this collar.

The choke chain is the usual collar recommended for training. It is constructed of highly polished steel so that it slides easily through the stainless steel loop. The idea is that the dog controls the pressure around its neck and he will stop pulling if the collar becomes uncomfortable. Never leave a choke collar on your dog when not training.

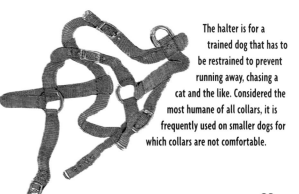

The halter is for a trained dog that has to be restrained to prevent running away, chasing a cat and the like. Considered the most humane of all collars, it is frequently used on smaller dogs for which collars are not comfortable.

Nylon leads are popular for everyday use. You should always walk your Westie on a lead, especially when he will be meeting other dogs.

LEAD

A 1- to 2-metre lead is recommended, preferably made of leather, nylon or heavy cloth. A chain lead is not recommended, as many dog owners find that the chain cuts into their hands and that frequently switching the lead back and forth between their hands is painful.

TREATS

Have a bag of treats on hand. Something nutritious and easy to swallow works best. Use a soft treat, a chunk of cheese or a piece of cooked chicken rather than a dry biscuit. By the time the dog gets done chewing a dry treat, he will forget why he is

Before you can teach your dog anything, you must have his attention...a food treat does wonders in making your Westie take notice!

94

DID YOU KNOW?
Training a dog is a life experience. Many parents admit that much of what they know about raising children they learned from caring for their dogs. Dogs respond to love, fairness and guidance, just as children do. Become a good dog owner and you may become an even better parent.

What dog doesn't love a snack? Using food as a training aid is often helpful in teaching new commands.

being rewarded in the first place! Using food rewards will not teach a dog to beg at the table— the only way to teach a dog to beg at the table is to give him food from the table. In training, rewarding the dog with a food treat will help him associate praise and the treats with learning new behaviours that obviously please his owner.

TRAINING BEGINS: ASK THE DOG A QUESTION

In order to teach your dog anything, you must first get his attention. After all, he cannot learn anything if he is looking away from you with his mind on something else.

To get his attention, ask him, 'School?' and immediately walk over to him and give him a treat as you tell him 'Good dog.' Wait a minute or two and repeat the routine, this time with a treat in your hand as you approach within

a foot of the dog. Do not go directly to him, but stop about a foot short of him and hold out the treat as you ask, 'School?' He will see you approaching with a treat in your hand and most likely

DID YOU KNOW?
The golden rule of dog training is simple. For each 'question' (command), there is only one correct answer (reaction). One command = one reaction. Keep practising the command until the dog reacts correctly without hesitating. Be repetitive but not monotonous. Dogs get bored just as people do!

begin walking toward you. As you meet, give him the treat and praise again.

The third time, ask the question, have a treat in your hand and walk only a short distance toward the dog so that he must walk almost all the way to you. As he reaches you, give him the treat and praise again.

By this time, the dog will probably be getting the idea that if he pays attention to you, especially when you ask that question, it will pay off in treats and fun activities for him. In other words, he learns that 'school' means doing fun things with you that result in treats and positive attention for him.

Remember that the dog does not understand your verbal

Placing light pressure on the dog's hindquarters will help ease him into the sit position as you are teaching the exercise.

DID YOU KNOW?

Dogs are sensitive to their master's moods and emotions. Use your voice wisely when communicating with your dog. Never raise your voice at your dog unless you are angry and trying to correct him. 'Barking' at your dog can become as meaningless as 'dogspeak' is to you. Think before you bark!

DID YOU KNOW?

Dogs do not understand our language. They can be trained to react to a certain sound, at a certain volume. If you say 'No, Oliver' in a very soft pleasant voice it will not have the same meaning as 'No, Oliver!!' when you shout it as loud as you can. You should never use the dog's name during a reprimand, just the command NO!! Since dogs don't understand words, comics use dogs trained with opposite meanings. Thus, when the comic commands his dog to SIT the dog will stand up; and vice versa.

All dogs need discipline, and they look to their owners to provide it.

language, he only recognises sounds. Your question translates to a series of sounds for him, and those sounds become the signal to go to you and pay attention; if he does, he will get to interact with you plus receive treats and praise.

THE BASIC COMMANDS
TEACHING SIT

Now that you have the dog's attention, attach his lead and hold it in your left hand and a food treat in your right. Place your food hand at the dog's nose and let him lick the treat but not take it from you. Say 'Sit' and slowly raise your food hand from in front of the dog's nose up over his head so that he is looking at the ceiling.

As he bends his head upward, he will have to bend his knees to maintain his balance. As he bends his knees, he will assume a sit position. At that point, release the food treat and praise lavishly with comments such as 'Good dog! Good sit!', etc. Remember to always praise enthusiastically, because dogs relish verbal praise from their owners and feel so proud of themselves whenever they accomplish a behaviour.

You will not use food forever in getting the dog to obey your commands. Food is only used to teach new behaviours, and once the dog knows what you want when you give a specific command, you will wean him off

Teaching your Westie to stay in either the sit or down position may require some patience but is usually not difficult.

of the food treats but still maintain the verbal praise. After all, you will always have your voice with you, and there will be many times when you have no food rewards but expect the dog to obey.

TEACHING DOWN

Teaching the down exercise is easy when you understand how the dog perceives the down position, and it is very difficult when you do not. Dogs perceive the down position as a submissive one, therefore teaching the down exercise using a forceful method can sometimes make the dog develop such a fear of the down that he either runs away when you say 'Down' or he attempts to bite the person who tries to force him down.

Have the dog sit close alongside your left leg, facing in the same direction as you are. Hold the lead in your left hand and a food treat in your right. Now place your left hand lightly on the top of the dog's shoulders where they meet above the spinal cord. Do not push down on the dog's shoulders; simply rest your left hand there so you can guide the dog to lie down close to your left leg rather than to swing away from your side when he drops.

Now place the food hand at the dog's nose, say 'Down' very softly (almost a whisper), and slowly lower the food hand to the dog's front feet. When the food hand reaches the floor, begin moving it forward along the floor in front of the dog. Keep talking softly to the dog, saying things like, 'Do you want this treat? You can do this, good dog.' Your reassuring tone of voice will help calm the dog as he tries to follow the food hand in order to get the treat.

When the dog's elbows touch the floor, release the food and praise softly. Try to get the dog to maintain that down position for several seconds before you let him sit up again. The goal here is to get the dog to settle down and not feel threatened in the down position.

TEACHING STAY

It is easy to teach the dog to stay in either a sit or a down position. Again, we use food and praise during the teaching process as we help the dog to understand exactly what it is that we are expecting him to do.

To teach the sit/stay, start with the dog sitting on your left side as before and hold the lead in your left hand. Have a food treat in your right hand and place your food hand at the dog's nose. Say 'Stay' and step out on your right foot to stand directly in front of the dog, toe to toe, as he licks and nibbles the treat. Be sure to keep his head facing upward to maintain the sit position. Count to five and then swing around to stand next to the dog again with him on your left. As soon as you get back to the original position, release the food and praise lavishly.

To teach the down/stay, do the down as previously described. As soon as the dog lies down, say 'Stay' and step out on your right foot just as you did in the sit/stay. Count to five and then return to stand beside the dog with him on your left side. Release the treat and praise as always.

Within a week or ten days, you can begin to add a bit of distance between you and your dog when you leave him. When you do, use your left hand open with the palm facing the dog as a stay signal, much the same as the hand signal a police officer uses to stop traffic at an intersection. Hold the food treat in your right hand as before, but this time the

It takes about a week or two to train your Westie to stay in the desired position. This discipline must be practised and reinforced frequently.

The 'Come' exercise should begin with the puppy as a game. This must be the most exciting fun for the puppy, because it is the most important of all lessons.

food is not touching the dog's nose. He will watch the food hand and quickly learn that he is going to get that treat as soon as you return to his side.

When you can stand 1 metre away from your dog for 30 seconds, you can then begin building time and distance in both stays. Eventually, the dog can be expected to remain in the stay position for prolonged periods of time until you return to him or call him to you. Always praise lavishly when he stays.

TEACHING COME
If you make teaching 'come' a fun experience, you should never have a 'student' that does not love the game or that fails to come when called. The secret, it seems, is never to teach the word 'come.'

At times when an owner most wants his dog to come when called, the owner is likely upset or anxious and he allows these feelings to come through in the tone of his voice when he calls his dog. Hearing that desperation in his owner's voice, the dog fears the results of going to him and therefore either disobeys outright or runs in the opposite direction. The secret, therefore, is to teach the dog a game and, when you want him to come to you, simply play the game. It is practically a no-fail solution!

To begin, have several members of your family take a few food treats and each go into a different room in the house. Take turns calling the dog, and each person should celebrate the dog's finding him with a treat and lots of happy praise. When a person calls the dog, he is actually inviting the dog to find him and

DID YOU KNOW?
Never call your dog to come to you for a correction or scold him when he reaches you. That is the quickest way to turn a 'Come' command into 'Go away fast!' Dogs think only in the present tense and he will connect the scolding with coming to his master, not with the misbehaviour of a few moments earlier.

but there are trainers who work with thousands of dogs and never teach the actual word 'Come.' Yet these dogs will race to respond to a person who uses the dog's name followed by 'Where are you?' For example, a woman has a 12-year-old companion dog who went blind, but who never fails to locate her owner when asked, 'Where are you?'

Children particularly love to play this game with their dogs. Children can hide in smaller places like a shower or bathtub, behind a bed or under a table. The dog needs to work a little bit harder to find these hiding places, but when he does he loves to celebrate with a treat and a tussle with a favourite youngster.

Dogs often anticipate the trainer's next command. Make training fun and rewarding for the puppy and your success is guaranteed.

get a treat as a reward for 'winning.'

A few turns of the 'Where are you?' game and the dog will figure out that everyone is playing the game and that each person has a big celebration awaiting his success at locating them. Once he learns to love the game, simply calling out 'Where are you?' will bring him running from wherever he is when he hears that all-important question.

The come command is recognised as one of the most important things to teach a dog,

This Westie has been commanded to sit/stay. He won't take his eyes from his master as he awaits the next command.

DID YOU KNOW?
When calling the dog, do not say 'Come.' Say things like, 'Rover, where are you? See if you can find me! I have a cookie for you!' Keep up a constant line of chatter with coaxing sounds and frequent questions such as, 'Where are you?' The dog will learn to follow the sound of your voice to locate you and receive his reward.

TEACHING HEEL

Heeling means that the dog walks beside the owner without pulling. It takes time and patience on the owner's part to succeed at

A properly trained dog must be taught to walk at your pace and at your side. Imagine how an untrained Westie would misbehave in this parade?

DID YOU KNOW?

If you are walking your dog and he suddenly stops and looks straight into your eyes, ignore him. Pull the leash and lead him into the direction you want to walk.

teaching the dog that he (the owner) will not proceed unless the dog is walking calmly beside him. Pulling out ahead on the lead is definitely not acceptable.

Begin with holding the lead in your left hand as the dog sits beside your left leg. Move the loop end of the lead to your right hand but keep your left hand short on the lead so it keeps the dog in close next to you.

Say 'Heel' and step forward on your left foot. Keep the dog

DID YOU KNOW?

If you begin teaching the heel by taking long walks and letting the dog pull you along, he misinterprets this action as an acceptable form of taking a walk. When you pull back on the lead to counteract his pulling, he reads that tug as a signal to pull even harder!

close to you and take three steps. Stop and have the dog sit next to you in what we now call the 'heel position.' Praise verbally, but do not touch the dog. Hesitate a moment and begin again with 'Heel,' taking three steps and stopping, at which point the dog is told to sit again.

Your goal here is to have the dog walk those three steps without pulling on the lead. When he will walk calmly beside you for three steps without pulling, increase the number of steps you take to five. When he will walk politely beside you whilst you take five steps, you can increase the length of your walk to ten steps. Keep increasing the length of your stroll until the dog will walk quietly beside you without pulling as long as you want him to heel. When you stop heeling, indicate to the dog that the exercise is over by verbally praising as you pet him and say 'OK, good dog.' The 'OK' is used as a release word meaning that the exercise is finished and the dog is

DID YOU KNOW?

Teach your dog to HEEL in an enclosed area. Once you think the dog will obey reliably and you want to attempt advanced obedience exercises such as off-lead heeling, test him in a fenced in area so he cannot run away.

within a few days he will be walking politely beside you without pulling on the lead. At first, the training sessions should be kept short and very positive; soon the dog will be able to walk nicely with you for increasingly longer distances. Remember also to give the dog free time and the opportunity to run and play when you are done with heel practice.

free to relax.

If you are dealing with a dog who insists on pulling you around, simply 'put on your brakes' and stand your ground until the dog realises that the two of you are not going anywhere until he is beside you and moving at your pace, not his. It may take some time just standing there to convince the dog that you are the leader and you will be the one to decide on the direction and speed of your travel.

Each time the dog looks up at you or slows down to give a slack lead between the two of you, quietly praise him and say, 'Good heel. Good dog.' Eventually, the dog will begin to respond and

Unless on a relief break, your Westie should walk alongside you on his lead and not pull far ahead.

DID YOU KNOW?

Your dog is actually training you at the same time you are training him. Dogs do things to get attention. They usually repeat whatever succeeds in getting your attention.

WEANING OFF FOOD IN TRAINING

Food is used in training new behaviours. Once the dog understands what behaviour goes with a specific command, it is time to start weaning him off the food treats. At first, give a treat after each exercise. Then, start to give a treat only after every other exercise. Mix up the times when you offer a food reward and the

Westies, like most other dogs, are very food motivated. It is sometimes difficult to quit food treats entirely, but it's helpful to practise without them once in a while.

times when you only offer praise so that the dog will never know when he is going to receive both food and praise and when he is going to receive only praise. This is called a variable ratio reward system and it proves successful because there is always the chance that the owner will produce a treat, so the dog never stops trying for that reward. No matter what, ALWAYS give verbal praise.

OBEDIENCE CLASSES

As previously discussed, it is a good idea to enrol in an obedience class if one is available in your

---

DID YOU KNOW?

Occasionally, a dog and owner who have not attended formal classes have been able to earn entry-level titles by obtaining competition rules and regulations from a local kennel club and practising on their own to a degree of perfection. Obtaining the higher level titles, however, almost always requires extensive training under the tutelage of experienced instructors. In addition, the more difficult levels require more specialised equipment whereas the lower levels do not.

area. Many areas have dog clubs that offer basic obedience training as well as preparatory classes for obedience competition. There are also local dog trainers who offer similar classes.

DID YOU KNOW?

A dog in jeopardy never lies down. He stays alert on his feet because instinct tells him that he may have to run away or fight for his survival. Therefore, if a dog feels threatened or anxious, he will not lie down. Consequently, it is important to have the dog calm and relaxed as he learns the down exercise.

DID YOU KNOW?

A basic obedience beginner's class usually lasts for six to eight weeks. Dog and owner attend an hour-long lesson once a week and practice for a few minutes, several times a day, each day at home. If done properly, the whole procedure will result in a well-mannered dog and an owner who delights in living with a pet that is eager to please and enjoys doing things with his owner.

At obedience trials, dogs can earn titles at various levels of competition. The beginning levels of competition include basic behaviours such as sit, down, heel, etc. The more advanced levels of competition include jumping, retrieving, scent discrimination and signal work. The advanced levels require a dog and owner to put a lot of time and effort into their training and the titles that can be earned at these levels of competition are very prestigious.

OTHER ACTIVITIES FOR LIFE

Whether a dog is trained in the structured environment of a class or alone with his owner at home, there are many activities that can bring fun and rewards to both owner and dog once they have mastered basic control.

Teaching the dog to help out around the home, in the garden or on the farm provides great satisfaction to both dog and owner. In addition, the dog's help makes life a little easier for his owner and raises his stature as a valued companion to his family. It helps give the dog a purpose by occupying his mind and providing an outlet for his energy.

Hiking is an exciting and healthful activity that the dog can be taught without assistance from more than his owner. The exercise of walking and climbing is good for man and dog alike, and the bond that they develop together is priceless.

If you are interested in participating in organised competition with your West Highland White Terrier, there are activities other than obedience in which you and your dog can become involved. Agility is a popular and fun sport where dogs run through an obstacle course that includes various jumps, tunnels and other exercises to test the dog's speed and coordination. The owners often run through the course beside their dogs to give commands and to guide them through the course. Although competitive, the focus is on fun—it's fun to do, fun to watch, and great exercise.

Dogs suffer many of the same physical illnesses as people. They might even share many of the same psychological problems. Since people usually know more about human diseases than canine maladies,

Establish a relationship with your chosen veterinary surgeon and have him examine your Westie on a regular basis. Ideally that may be every six months, but certainly not less than once a year.

many of the terms used in this chapter will be familiar but not necessarily those used by veterinary surgeons. We will use the term *x-ray,* instead of the more acceptable term *radiograph.* We will also use the familiar term *symptoms* even though dogs don't have symptoms, which are verbal descriptions of the patient's feelings: dogs have *clinical signs.* Since dogs can't

speak, we have to look for clinical signs...but we still use the term symptoms in this book.

As a general rule, medicine is practised. That term is not arbitrary. Medicine is a constantly changing art as we learn more and more about genetics, electronic aids (like CAT scans) and daily laboratory advances. There are many dog maladies, like canine hip dysplasia, which are not universally treated in the same manner. Some veterinary surgeons opt for surgery more often than others do.

SELECTING A VET
Your selection of a veterinary surgeon should not be based upon personality (as most are) but upon their convenience to your home. You want a doctor who is close because you might have emergencies or need to make multiple visits for treatments. You want a doctor who has services that you might require such as a boarding kennel and grooming facilities, as well as sophisticated pet supplies and a good reputation for ability and responsiveness. There is nothing

more frustrating than having to wait a day or more to get a response from your veterinary surgeon.

All veterinary surgeons are licensed and their diplomas and/or certificates should be displayed in their waiting rooms. There are, however, many veterinary specialities that usually require further studies and internships. There are specialists in heart problems (veterinary cardiologists), skin problems (veterinary dermatologists), teeth and gum problems (veterinary dentists), eye problems (veterinary ophthalmologists), X-rays (veterinary radiologists), and surgeons who have specialities in bones, muscles or other organs. Most veterinary surgeons do routine surgery such as neutering, stitching up wounds and docking tails for those breeds in which such is required for show purposes. When the problem affecting your dog is serious, it is not unusual or impudent to get another medical opinion. You might also want to compare costs amongst several veterinary surgeons. Sophisticated health care and veterinary services can be very costly. Don't be bashful about discussing these costs with your veterinary surgeon or his (her) staff. It is not infrequent that important decisions are based upon financial considerations.

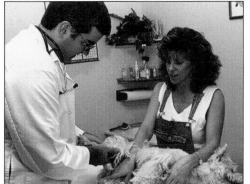

If your dog starts to act abnormal and you suspect he is ill, take him to the vet for an evaluation. Never hesitate to call and make an appointment if your dog is sick.

PREVENTATIVE MEDICINE

It is much easier, less costly and more effective to practise preventative medicine than to fight bouts of illness and disease. Properly bred puppies come from parents that were selected based upon their genetic disease profile. Their mothers should have been vaccinated, free of all internal and external parasites, and properly nourished. For these reasons, a visit to the veterinary surgeon who cared for the dam (mother) is recommended. The dam can pass on disease resistance to her puppies, which can last for eight to ten weeks. She can also pass on parasites and many infections. That's why you should visit the veterinary surgeon who cared for the dam.

WEANING TO FIVE MONTHS OLD

Puppies should be weaned by the time they are about two months old. A puppy that remains for at least eight weeks

107

with its mother and litter mates usually adapts better to other dogs and people later in its life.

In every case, you should have your newly acquired puppy examined by a veterinary surgeon immediately. Vaccination programmes usually begin when the puppy is very young.

The puppy will have its teeth examined and have its skeletal conformation and general health checked prior to certification by the veterinary surgeon. Many puppies have problems with their kneecaps, eye cataracts and other eye problems, heart murmurs and undescended testicles. They may also have personality problems and your veterinary surgeon might have training in temperament evaluation.

VACCINATION SCHEDULING
Most vaccinations are given by injection and should only be done by a veterinary surgeon. Both he and you should keep a record of the date of the injection, the identification of the vaccine and the amount given. The first vaccinations

HEALTH AND VACCINATION SCHEDULE

AGE IN WEEKS:	3RD	6TH	8TH	10TH	12TH	14TH	16TH	20-24TH
Worm Control	✔	✔	✔	✔	✔	✔	✔	✔
Neutering								✔
Heartworm		✔						✔
Parvovirus		✔		✔		✔		✔
Distemper			✔		✔		✔	
Hepatitis			✔		✔		✔	
Leptospirosis		✔		✔		✔		
Parainfluenza		✔		✔		✔		
Dental Examination			✔					✔
Complete Physical			✔					✔
Temperament Testing			✔					
Coronavirus					✔			
Kennel Cough		✔						
Hip Dysplasia							✔	
Rabies								✔

Vaccinations are not instantly effective. It takes about two weeks for the dog's immune system to develop antibodies. Most vaccinations require annual booster shots. Your veterinary surgeon should guide you in this regard.

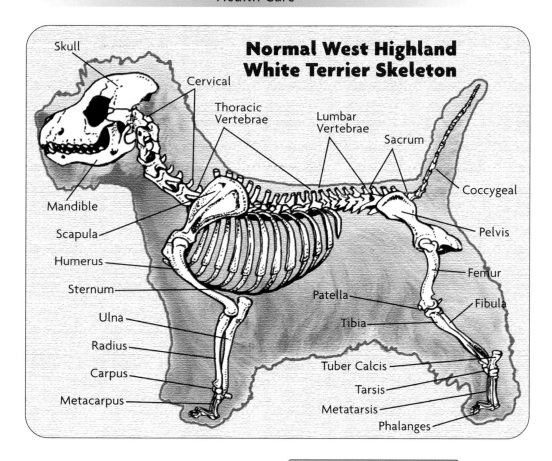

Normal West Highland White Terrier Skeleton

Skull

Cervical

Thoracic Vertebrae

Lumbar Vertebrae

Sacrum

Coccygeal

Mandible

Scapula

Humerus

Sternum

Ulna

Radius

Carpus

Metacarpus

Pelvis

Femur

Patella

Fibula

Tibia

Tuber Calcis

Tarsis

Metatarsis

Phalanges

should start when the puppy is 6–8 weeks old, the second when it is 10–12 weeks of age and the third when it is 14–16 weeks of age. Vaccinations should never be given without a 15-day lapse between injections. Most vaccinations immunise your puppy against viruses.

The usual vaccines contain immunising doses of several different viruses such as distemper, parvovirus, parainfluenza and hepatitis. There are other

DID YOU KNOW?

Vaccines do not work all the time. Sometimes dogs are allergic to them and many times the antibodies, which are supposed to be stimulated by the vaccine, just are not produced. You should keep your dog in the veterinary clinic for an hour after it is vaccinated to be sure there are no allergic reactions.

Disease	What is it?	What causes it?	Symptoms
Leptospirosis	Severe disease that affects the internal organs; can be spread to people.	A bacterium, which is often carried by rodents, that enters through mucous membranes and spreads quickly throughout the body.	Range from fever, vomiting and loss of appetite in less severe cases to shock, irreversible kidney damage and possibly death in most severe cases.
Rabies	Potentially deadly virus that infects warm-blooded mammals. Not seen in United Kingdom.	Bite from a carrier of the virus, mainly wild animals.	1st stage: dog exhibits change in behaviour, fear. 2nd stage: dog's behaviour becomes more aggressive. 3rd stage: loss of coordination, trouble with bodily functions.
Parvovirus	Highly contagious virus, potentially deadly.	Ingestion of the virus, which is usually spread through the faeces of infected dogs.	Most common: severe diarrhoea. Also vomiting, fatigue, lack of appetite.
Kennel cough	Contagious respiratory infection.	Combination of types of bacteria and virus. Most common: *Bordetella bronchiseptica* bacteria and parainfluenza virus.	Chronic cough.
Distemper	Disease primarily affecting respiratory and nervous system.	Virus that is related to the human measles virus.	Mild symptoms such as fever, lack of appetite and mucous secretion progress to evidence of brain damage, 'hard pad.'
Hepatitis	Virus primarily affecting the liver.	Canine adenovirus type I (CAV-1). Enters system when dog breathes in particles.	Lesser symptoms include listlessness, diarrhoea, vomiting. More severe symptoms include 'blue-eye' (clumps of virus in eye).
Coronavirus	Virus resulting in digestive problems.	Virus is spread through infected dog's faeces.	Stomach upset evidenced by lack of appetite, vomiting, diarrhoea.

vaccines available when the puppy is at risk. You should rely upon professional advice. This is especially true for the booster-shot programme. Most vaccination programmes require a booster when the puppy is a year old and once a year thereafter. In some cases, circumstances may require more frequent immunisations. Canine cough, more formally known as tracheobronchitis, is treated with a vaccine that is sprayed into the dog's nostrils.

The effectiveness of a parvovirus vaccination programme can be tested using the parvovirus antibody titer to be certain that the vaccinations are protective. Your veterinary surgeon will explain and manage all of these details.

FIVE MONTHS TO ONE YEAR
By the time your puppy is five

DID YOU KNOW?
Feeding your dog properly is very important. An incorrect diet could affect the dog's health, behaviour and nervous system, possibly making a normal dog into an aggressive one.

months old, he should have completed his vaccination programme. During his physical examination he should be evaluated for the common hip dysplasia and other diseases of the joints. There are tests to assist in the prediction of these problems. Other tests can be run to assess the effectiveness of the vaccination programme.

Unless you intend to breed or show your dog, neutering the puppy at six months of age is recommended. Discuss this with your veterinary surgeon; most professionals advise neutering the puppy. Neutering has proven to be extremely beneficial to both male and female puppies. Besides eliminating the possibility of pregnancy, it inhibits (but does not prevent) breast cancer in bitches and prostate cancer in male dogs.

DOGS OLDER THAN ONE YEAR

Continue to visit the veterinary surgeon at least once a year. There is no such disease as old age, but bodily functions do change with age. The eyes and ears are no longer as efficient. Liver, kidney and intestinal functions often decline. Proper dietary changes, recommended by your veterinary surgeon, can make life more pleasant for the ageing West Highland White Terrier and you.

DID YOU KNOW?
A dental examination is in order when the dog is between six months and one year of age so any permanent teeth that have erupted incorrectly can be corrected. It is important to begin a brushing routine, preferably using a two-sided brushing technique, whereby both sides of the tooth are brushed at the same time. Durable nylon and safe edible chews should be a part of your puppy's arsenal for good health, good teeth and pleasant breath. The vast majority of dogs three to four years old and older has diseases of their gums from lack of dental attention. Using the various types of dental chews can be very effective in controlling dental plaque.

SKIN PROBLEMS IN WEST HIGHLAND WHITE TERRIERS

Veterinary surgeons are consulted by dog owners for skin problems more than any other group of diseases or maladies. Dogs' skin is almost as sensitive as human skin and both suffer almost the same ailments (though the occurrence of acne in dogs is rare!). For this reason, veterinary dermatology has developed into a speciality practised by many veterinary surgeons.

Since many skin problems have visual symptoms that are

DID YOU KNOW?

Your veterinary surgeon will probably recommend that your puppy be vaccinated before you take him outside. There are airborne diseases, parasite eggs in the grass and unexpected visits from other dogs that might be dangerous to your puppy's health.

almost identical, it requires the skill of an experienced veterinary dermatologist to identify and cure many of the more severe skin disorders. Pet shops sell many treatments for skin problems but most of the treatments are directed at symptoms and not the underlying problem(s). If your dog is suffering from a skin disorder, you should seek professional assistance as quickly as possible. As with all diseases, the earlier a problem is identified and treated, the more successful is the cure.

INHERITED SKIN PROBLEMS

Many skin disorders are inherited and some are fatal. In West Highland White Terriers, epidermal dysplasia is most commonly found. Young puppies manifest dark-coloured skin and are very itchy. The dark, thickened skin appears dry but greasy, like a dog suffering from bad allergies.

Diagnosis is accomplished by skin biopsies, and only experienced dermatologist are qualified to identify epidermal dysplasia. There is no known cure, but vets prescribe potent topical and oral medications to control the discomfort. Affected dogs (and their relatives) should not be bred.

Less common in Westies, Acrodermatitis is an inherited disease that is transmitted by both parents. The parents, who appear (phenotypically) normal, have a recessive gene for acrodermatitis, meaning that they carry, but are not affected by the disease.

Acrodermatitis is just one example of how difficult it is to prevent congenital dog diseases. The cost and skills required to ascertain whether two dogs should be mated are too high even though puppies with acrodermatitis rarely reach two years of age.

DID YOU KNOW?

Chances are that you and your dog will have the same allergies. Your allergies are readily recognizable and usually easily treated. Your dog's allergies may be masked.

Other inherited skin problems are usually not as fatal as acrodermatitis. All inherited diseases must be diagnosed and treated by a veterinary specialist. There are active programmes being undertaken by many veterinary pharmaceutical manufacturers to solve most, if not all, of the common skin problems of dogs.

PARASITE BITES

Many of us are allergic to mosquito bites. The bites itch, erupt and may even become infected. Dogs have the same reaction to fleas, ticks and/or mites. When you feel the prick of the mosquito as it bites you, you have a chance to kill it with your hand. Unfortunately, when our dog is bitten by a flea, tick or mite, it can only scratch it away or bite it. By the time the dog has been bitten, the parasite has done some of its damage. It may also have laid eggs to cause further problems in the near future. The itching from parasite bites is probably due to the saliva injected into the site when the parasite sucks the dog's blood.

AUTO-IMMUNE SKIN CONDITIONS

Auto-immune skin conditions are commonly referred to as being allergic to yourself, whilst allergies are usually inflammatory reactions to an outside stimulus. Auto-immune diseases cause serious damage to the tissues that are involved.

The best known auto-immune disease is lupus, which affects people as well as dogs. The symptoms are variable and may affect the kidneys, bones, blood chemistry and skin. It can be fatal to both dogs and humans, though it is not thought to be transmissible. It is usually successfully treated with cortisone, prednisone or similar corticosteroid, but extensive use

PET ADVANTAGES

If you do not intend to show or breed your new puppy, your veterinary surgeon will probably recommend that you spay your female or neuter your male. Some people believe neutering leads to weight gain, but if you feed and exercise your dog properly, this is easily avoided. Spaying or neutering can actually have many positive outcomes, such as:

• training becomes easier, as the dog focuses less on the urge to mate and more on you!

• females are protected from unplanned pregnancy as well as ovarian and uterine cancers.

• males are guarded from testicular tumours and have a reduced risk of developing prostate cancer.

Talk to your vet regarding the right age to spay/neuter and other aspects of the procedure.

Of course all dogs that spend time outdoors are subject to parasite infestation, insect bites and airborne allergies.

pollen and house dust allergies.

Dogs, like humans, can be tested for allergens. Discuss the testing with your veterinary dermatologist. Westies suffering from inflammation due to allergies tend to exhibit darker skin, developing from red to a blackish colour.

of these drugs can have harmful side effects.

AIRBORNE ALLERGIES

West Highland White Terriers show greater tendency toward inhalant allergies than other breeds. The usual offender include pollen, dust and moulds. Humans have hay fever, rose fever and other fevers with which they suffer during the pollinating season. Many dogs suffer the same allergies. When the pollen count is high, your dog might suffer but don't expect them to sneeze and have runny noses like humans. Dogs react to pollen allergies the same way they react to fleas—they scratch and bite themselves. Westies tend to rub their faces with their front feet, lick and bite at their front feet, and develop rashes on their bellies or in the armpits. West Highland White Terriers are very susceptible to airborne

FOOD PROBLEMS
FOOD ALLERGIES

Dogs can be allergic to many foods that are best-sellers and highly recommended by breeders and veterinary surgeons. Changing the brand of food that you buy may not eliminate the problem if the element to which the dog is allergic is contained in the new brand.

Recognising a food allergy is difficult. Humans vomit or have rashes when they eat a food to which they are allergic. Dogs neither vomit nor (usually) develop a rash. They react in the same manner as they do to an airborne or flea allergy: they itch, scratch and bite, thus making the diagnosis extremely difficult. Whilst pollen allergies and parasite bites are usually seasonal, food allergies are year-round problems.

FOOD INTOLERANCE

Food intolerance is the inability of the dog to completely digest certain foods. Puppies that may have done very well on their mother's milk may not do well on cow's milk. The result of this food intolerance may be loose bowels, passing gas and stomach pains. These are the only obvious symptoms of food intolerance and that makes diagnosis difficult.

TREATING FOOD PROBLEMS

It is possible to handle food allergies and food intolerance yourself. Put your dog on a diet that it has never had. Obviously if it has never eaten this new food it can't have been allergic or intolerant of it. Start with a single ingredient that is not in the dog's diet at the present time. Ingredients like chopped beef or fish are common in dog's diets, so try something more exotic like ostrich, rabbit,

> **DID YOU KNOW?**
> Your dog's protein needs are changeable. High activity level, stress, climate and other physical factors may require your dog to have more protein in his diet. Check with your veterinary surgeon.

> **DID YOU KNOW?**
> Feeding your dog properly is very important. An incorrect diet could affect the dog's health, behaviour and nervous system, possibly making a normal dog into an aggressive one.

pheasant or even just vegetables. Keep the dog on this diet (with no additives) for a month. If the symptoms of food allergy or intolerance disappear, chances are your dog has a food allergy.

Don't think that the single ingredient cured the problem. You still must find a suitable diet and ascertain which ingredient in the old diet was objectionable. This is most easily done by adding ingredients to the new diet one at a time. Let the dog stay on the modified diet for a month before you add another ingredient. Eventually, you will determine the ingredient that caused the adverse reaction.

An alternative method is to carefully study the ingredients in the diet to which your dog is allergic or intolerable. Identify the main ingredient in this diet and eliminate the main ingredient by buying a different food that does not have that ingredient. Keep experimenting until the symptoms disappear after one month on the new diet.

A scanning electron micrograph (S. E. M.) of a dog flea, *Ctenocephalides canis.*

S. E. M. BY DR DENNIS KUNKEL, UNIVERSITY OF HAWAII

(Facing Page) A scanning electron micrograph of a dog or cat flea, *Ctenocephalides,* magnified more than 100x. This has been colourised for effect.

EXTERNAL PARASITES

Of all the problems to which dogs are prone, none is more well known and frustrating than fleas. Fleas, as well as ticks and mites, are difficult to prevent but relatively simple to cure. Parasites that are

Magnified head of a dog flea, *Ctenocephalides canis.*

DID YOU KNOW?

Fleas have been around for millions of years and have adapted to changing host animals.

They are able to go through a complete life cycle in less than one month or they can extend their lives to almost two years by remaining as pupae or cocoons. They do not need blood or any other food for up to 20 months.

They have been measured as being able to jump 300,000 times and can jump 150 times their length in any direction including straight up. Those are just a few of the reasons they are so successful in infesting a dog!

harboured inside the body are more difficult to cure but they are easier to control.

FLEAS

To control a flea infestation you have to understand the life cycle of a typical flea. Fleas are basically a summertime problem and their effective treatment (destruction) is environmental. There is no single flea-control medicine (insecticide) that can be used in every flea-infested area. To understand flea control you must apply suitable treatment to the weak link in the life cycle of the flea.

THE LIFE CYCLE OF A FLEA

Fleas are found in four forms: eggs, larvae, pupae and adults. You really need a low-power microscope or hand lens to identify a living flea's eggs, pupae or larva. They spend

S. E. M. BY DR DENNIS KUNKEL, UNIVERSITY OF HAWAII

S. E. M. BY DR DENNIS KUNKEL, UNIVERSITY OF HAWAII

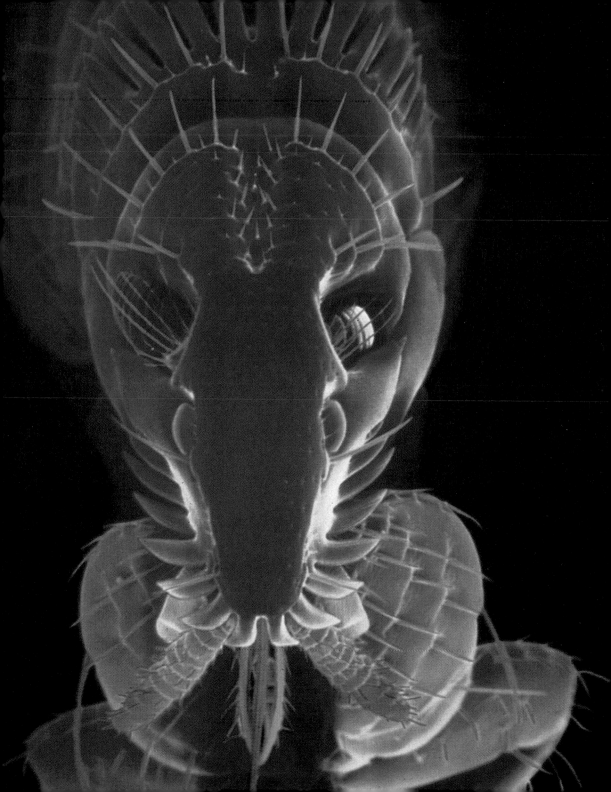

The Life Cycle of the Flea

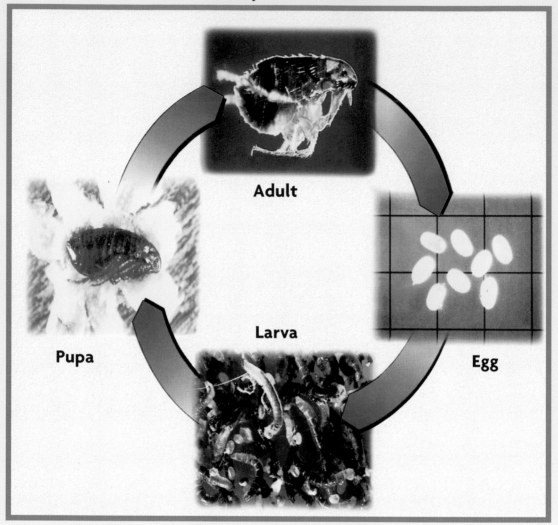

Adult

Pupa

Larva

Egg

their whole lives on your dog unless they are forcibly removed by brushing, bathing, scratching or biting.

The dog flea is scientifically known as *Ctenocephalides canis* whilst the cat flea is called *Ctenocephalides felis*. Several species infest both dogs and cats.

Fleas lay eggs whilst they are in residence upon your dog. These eggs fall off almost as

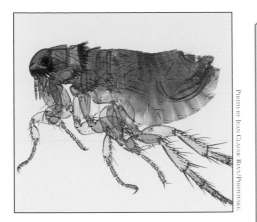

PHOTO BY JEAN CLAUDE REVY/PHOTOTAKE

There are many parasiticides which can be used around your home and garden to control fleas.

Natural pyrethrins can be used inside the house.

Allethrin, bioallethrin, permethrin and resmethrin can also be used inside the house but permethrin has been used successfully outdoors, too.

Carbaryl can be used indoors and outdoors.

Propoxur can be used indoors.

Chlorpyrifos, diazinon and malathion can be used indoors or outdoors and it has an extended residual activity.

A male dog flea, *Ctenocephalides canis.*

soon as they dry (they may be a bit damp when initially laid) and are the reservoir of future flea infestations. If your dog scratches himself and is able to dislodge a few fleas, they simply fall off and await a future chance to attack a dog...or even a person. Yes, fleas from dogs bite people. That's why it is so important to control fleas both on the dog and in the dog's entire environment. You must, therefore, treat the dog and the environment simultaneously.

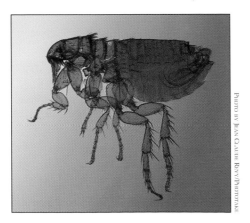

PHOTO BY JEAN CLAUDE REVY/PHOTOTAKE

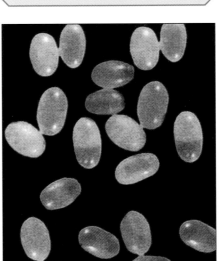

The eggs of the dog flea.

Male cat fleas, *Ctenocephalides felis*, are very commonly found on dogs.

119

Dwight R. Kuhn's magnificent action photo showing a flea jumping from a dog's back.

dogs (like window sills, table tops, etc.), so you have to clean all of these areas. The hard floor surfaces (tiles, wood, stone and linoleum) must be mopped several times a day. Drops of food onto the floor are actually food for flea larvae! All rugs and furniture must be vacuumed several times a day. Don't forget closets, under furniture and cushions. A study has reported that a vacuum cleaner with a beater bar can remove only

DE-FLEAING THE HOME

Cleanliness is the simple rule. If you have a cat living with your dog, the matter is more complicated since most dog fleas are actually cat fleas. Cats climb onto many areas that are never accessible to

Human lice look like dog lice; the two are closely related.

DID YOU KNOW?

Ivermectin is quickly becoming the drug of choice for treating many parasitic skin diseases in dogs.

For some unknown reason, herding dogs like Collies, Old English Sheepdogs and German Shepherds, etc., are extremely sensitive to ivermectin.

Ivermectin injections have killed some dogs, but dogs heavily infected with skin disorders may be treated anyway.

The ivermectin reaction is a toxicosis that causes tremors, loss of power to move their muscles, prolonged dilatation of the pupil of the eye, coma (unconsciousness), or cessation of breathing (death).

The toxicosis usually starts from 4-6 hours after ingestion (not injection), but can begin as late as 12 hours. The longer it takes to set in, the milder is the reaction.

Ivermectin should only be prescribed and administered by a vet.

Some ivermectin treatments require two doses.

DID YOU KNOW?
Never mix flea control products without first consulting your veterinary surgeon. Some products can become toxic when combined with others and can cause serious or fatal consequences.

mops, you have to treat the outdoor range of your dog. When trimming bushes and spreading insecticide, be careful not to poison areas in which fishes or other animals reside. Remember to choose dog-safe insecticides, but to be absolutely sure, keep your dog away from treated areas.

20 percent of the larvae and 50 percent of the eggs. The vacuum bags should be discarded into a sealed plastic bag or burned. The vacuum machine itself should be cleaned. The outdoor area to which your dog has access must also be treated with an insecticide.

Your vet will be able to recommend a household insecticidal spray, but this must be used with caution and instructions strictly adhered to.

There are many drugs available to kill fleas on the dog itself, such as the miracle drug ivermectin, and it is best to have the de-fleaing and de-worming supervised by your vet. Ivermectin is effective against many external and internal parasites including heartworms, roundworms, tapeworms, flukes, ticks and mites. It has not been approved for use to control these pests, but veterinary surgeons frequently use it anyway. Ivermectin may not be available in all areas.

STERILISING THE ENVIRONMENT
Besides cleaning your home with vacuum cleaners and

DID YOU KNOW?
There are drugs which prevent fleas from maturing from egg to adult.

The weak link is the maturation from a larva to a pupa.

Methoprene and fenoxycarb mimic the effect of maturation enhancers, thus, in effect, killing the larva before it pupates.

Methoprene is very effective in killing flea eggs while fenoxycarb is better able to stand UV rays from the sun. There is a combination of both drugs which has an effective life of 6 months and destroys 93% of the flea population.

It is important, in order to effectively control fleas, that you use products designed to kill fleas at all stages of growth, Manufacturers make such products, which are specifically designed for this purpose, and specially made to be safe for use in the home and on the dog.

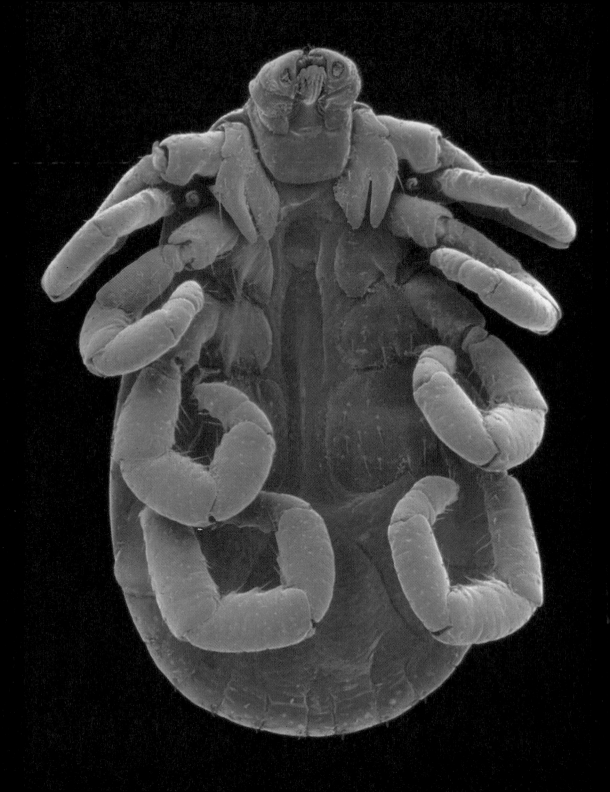

TICKS AND MITES

Though not as common as fleas, ticks and mites are found all over the tropical and temperate world. They don't bite like fleas, they harpoon. They dig their sharp proboscis (nose) into the dog's skin and drink the blood, which is their only food and drink. Dogs can get paralysis, Lyme disease, Rocky Mountain spotted fever (normally found in the U.S.A. only), and many other diseases from ticks and mites. They may live where fleas are found but they also like to hide in cracks or seams in walls wherever dogs live. They are controlled the same way fleas are controlled.

The tick *Dermacentor variabilis* may well be the most common dog tick in many geographical areas, especially where the climate is hot and humid.

Most dog ticks have life expectancies of a week to six months, depending upon climatic conditions. They neither jump nor fly, but crawl slowly and can range up to 5 metres 16 feet) to reach a sleeping or unsuspecting dog.

MANGE

Mange is a skin irritation caused by mites. Some mites are

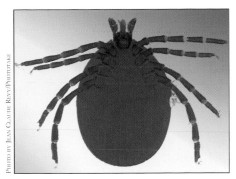

PHOTO BY JEAN CLAUDE REVY/PHOTOTAKE

An uncommon dog tick of the genus *Ixode*. Magnified 10x.

contagious, like *Cheyletiella*, ear mites, scabies and chiggers. The non-contagious mites are *Demodex*. The most serious of the mites is the one that causes ear-mite infestation. Ear mites are usually controlled with ivermectin.

It is essential that your dog be treated for mange as quickly as possible because some forms of mange are transmissible to people.

(Facing Page) The dog tick, *Dermacentor variabilis*, is probably the most common tick found on dogs. Look at the strength in its eight legs! No wonder it's hard to detach them.

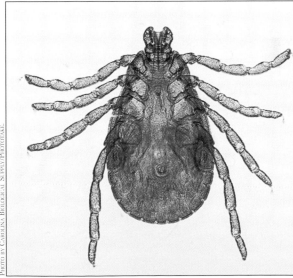

PHOTO BY CAROLINA BIOLOGICAL SUPPLY/PHOTOTAKE

A brown dog tick, *Rhipicephalus sanguineus*, is an uncommon but annoying tick found on dogs.

123

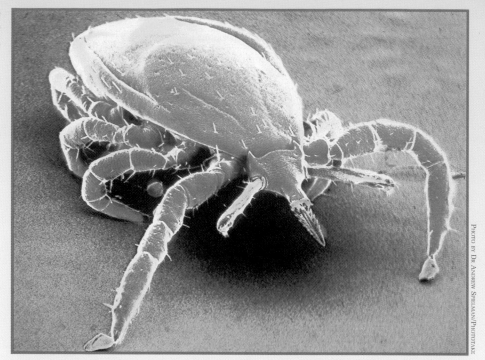

A deer tick, the carrier of Lyme disease.

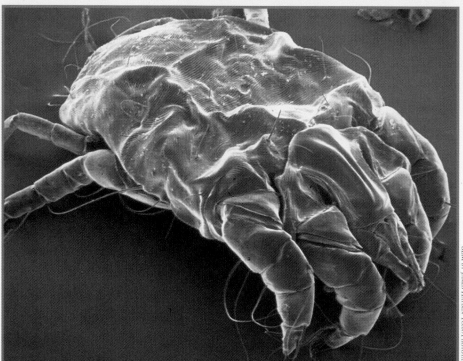

Magnified view of the mange mite, *Psoroptes bovis.*

INTERNAL PARASITES

Most animals—fishes, birds and mammals, including dogs and humans—have worms and other parasites that live inside their bodies. According to Dr Herbert R. Axelrod, the fish pathologist, there are two kinds of parasites: dumb and smart. The smart parasites live in peaceful cooperation with their hosts (symbiosis), whilst the dumb parasites kill their host. Most of the worm infections are relatively easy to control. If they are not controlled they eventually weaken the host dog to the point that other medical problems occur, but they are not dumb parasites that directly cause the death of their hosts.

ROUNDWORMS

The roundworms that infect dogs are scientifically known as *Toxocara canis.* They live in the dog's intestine and shed eggs continually. It has been estimated that an average-sized dog produces about 150 grammes of faeces every day. Each gramme of faeces averages 10,000–12,000 eggs of roundworms. All areas in which dogs

DID YOU KNOW?

Ridding your puppy of worms is VERY IMPORTANT because certain worms that puppies carry, such as tapeworms and roundworms, can infect humans.

Breeders initiate a deworming programme at or about four weeks of age. The routine is repeated every two or three weeks until the puppy is three months old. The breeder from whom you obtained your puppy should provide you with the complete details of the deworming programme.

Your veterinary surgeon can prescribe and monitor the programme of deworming for you. The usual programme is treating the puppy every 15 to 20 days until the puppy is positively worm free.

It is not advised that you treat your puppy with drugs that are not recommended professionally.

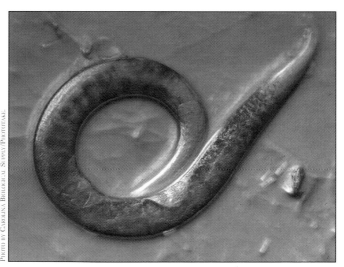

Photo by Carolina Biological Supply/Phototake.

The roundworm can infect both dogs and humans.

The roundworm *Rhabditis*.

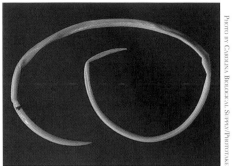

PHOTO BY CAROLINA BIOLOGICAL SUPPLY/PHOTOTAKE

PHOTO BY DWIGHT R KUHN

Male and female hookworms, *Ancylostoma caninum*, are uncommonly found in pet or show dogs in Britain. Hookworms may infect other dogs that have exposure to grasslands.

roam contain astronomical numbers of roundworm eggs. The greatest danger of roundworms is that they infect people, too! It is wise to have your dog tested regularly for roundworms.

Pigs also have roundworm infections that can be passed to human and dogs. The typical pig roundworm parasite is called *Ascaris lumbricoides*.

HOOKWORMS

The worm *Ancylostoma caninum* is commonly called the dog hookworm. It is also dangerous to humans and cats. It attaches itself

DID YOU KNOW?

Caring for the puppy starts before the puppy is born by keeping the dam healthy and well-nourished. Most puppies have worms, even if they are not evident, so a worming programme is essential. The worms continually shed eggs except during their dormant stage, when they just rest in the tissues of the puppy. During this stage they are not evident during a routine examination.

to the dog's intestines by its teeth. It changes the site of its attachment about six times a day, and the dog loses blood from each detachment. This blood loss can cause iron-deficiency anaemia. Hookworms are easily purged from the dog with many medications, the best of which seems to be ivermectin even though it has not been approved for such use.

In Britain the 'temperate climate' hookworm (*Uncinaria stenocephala*) is rarely found in pet or show dogs, but can occur in hunting packs, racing Greyhounds and sheepdogs because these hookworms can be prevalent wherever dogs are exercised regularly on grassland.

DID YOU KNOW?

Average size dogs can pass 1,360,000 roundworm eggs every day.

For example, if there were only 1 million dogs in the world, the world would be saturated with 1,300 metric tonnes of dog faeces. These faeces would contain 15,000,000,000 roundworm eggs.

7 to 31 percent of home gardens and children's play boxes in the U. S. contained roundworm eggs.

Flushing dog's faeces down the toilet is not a safe practice because the usual sewage treatments do not destroy roundworm eggs.

Infected puppies start shedding roundworm eggs at 3 weeks of age. They can be infected by their mother's milk.

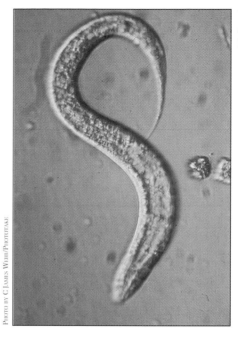

The infective stage of the hookworm larva.

PHOTO BY C. JAMES WEBB/PHOTOTAKE

TAPEWORMS

There are many species of tapeworms, many of which are carried by fleas! The dog eats the flea and starts the tapeworm cycle. Humans can also be infected with tapeworms, so don't eat fleas! Fleas are so small that your dog could pass them onto your hands, your plate or your food and make it possible for you to ingest a flea which is carrying tapeworm eggs.

Whilst tapeworm infection is not life threatening in dogs (smart parasite!), it can be the cause of a very serious liver disease for humans. About 50 percent of the humans infected with *Echinococcus multilocularis*, causing alveolar hydatis, perish.

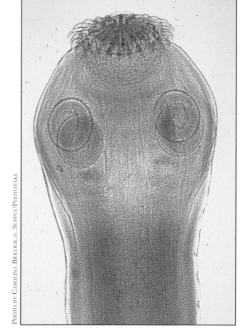

The head and rostellum (the round prominence on the scolex) of a tapeworm, which infects dogs and humans.

PHOTO BY CAROLINA BIOLOGICAL SUPPLY/PHOTOTAKE

DID YOU KNOW?

Humans, rats, squirrels, foxes, coyotes, wolves, mixed breeds of dogs and purebred dogs are all susceptible to tapeworm infection. Except in humans, tapeworms are usually not a fatal infection. Infected individuals can harbour a thousand parasitic worms. Tapeworms have two sexes—male and female (many other worms have only one sex—male and female in the same worm). If dogs eat infected rats or mice, they get the tapeworm disease.

One month after attaching to a dog's intestine, the worm starts shedding eggs. These eggs are infective immediately. Infective eggs can live for a few months without a host animal. Roundworms, whipworms and tapeworms are just a few of the other commonly known worms that infect dogs.

HEARTWORMS

Heartworms are thin, extended worms up to 30 cms (12 ins) long that live in a dog's heart and the major blood vessels around it. Your pet may have up to 200 of these worms. The symptoms may be loss of energy, loss of appetite, coughing, the development of a pot belly and anaemia.

Heartworms are transmitted by mosquitoes. The mosquito drinks the blood of an infected dog and takes in larvae with the blood. The larvae, called microfilaria, develop within the body of the mosquito and are passed on to the next dog bitten after the larvae mature. It takes two to three weeks for the larvae to develop to the infective stage within the body of the mosquito. Dogs should be treated at about six weeks of age, then every six months.

Blood testing for heartworms is not necessarily indicative of how seriously your dog is infected. This is a dangerous disease. Dogs in the United Kingdom are not affected by heartworm.

The heartworm, *Dirofilaria immitis.*

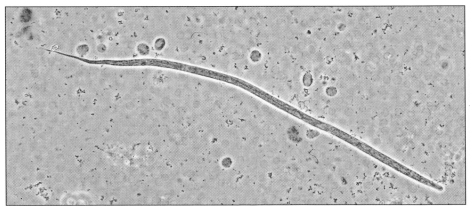

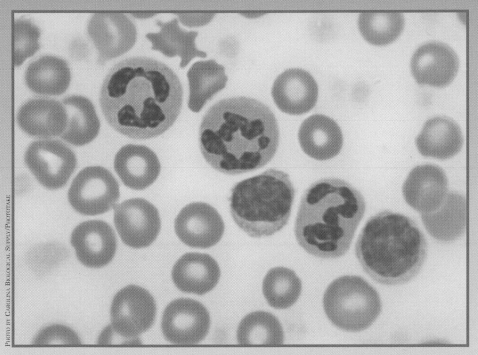

Magnified
heartworm
larvae,
*Dirofilaria
immitis.*

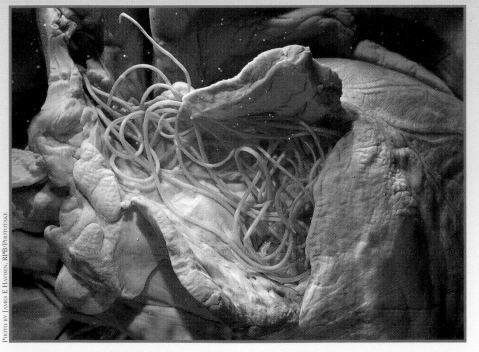

The heart
of a dog infected
with canine
heartworm,
*Dirofilaria
immitis.*

MEDICAL PROBLEMS
MOST FREQUENTLY SEEN IN WEST HIGHLAND WHITE TERRIERS

Condition	Age Affected	Cause	Area Affected
Aortic Stenosis	Young pups	Congenital	Heart
Cataracts (cloudiness on lens)	Before 1 year	Congenital	Eyes
Copper Toxicosis	Adults	Congenital	Liver
Craniomandibular Osteopathy	4 to 7 mos	Congenital	Bones of lower jaw, inner ear, head
Elbow Dysplasia	4 to 7 mos	Congenital	Elbow joint (forequarter lameness)
Epidermal Dysplasia	Young pups	Congenital	Skin
Gastric Dilatation (Bloat)	Older dogs	Swallowing air	Stomach
Globoid Cell Leukodystrophy	11 to 30 weeks	Congenital	Neurological
Hip Dysplasia	By 2 years	Congenital	Hip joint
Hypothyroidism	1 to 3 years	Congenital	Endocrine system
Inhalant Allergies	After 6 months	Atmospheric	Skin reactions
Keratoconjunctivitis Sicca	Any age	Drug reactions	Eyes
Legg-Calve-Perthes Disease	4 to 10 months	Injury/diet	Leg (hindquarter lameness)
Liver Disease	2 to 4 years	Congenital	Liver
Medical Patellar Luxation	Any age	Poss. congenital	Slipped kneecap
Osteochondrosis	4 to 7 months	Congenital	Cartilage (forequarter lameness)
Primary Glaucoma	Over 5 years	Hereditary	Eyes (blindness)
Von Willebrand's Disease	Birth	Congenital	Blood

West Highland White Terrier

The term old is a qualitative term. For dogs, as well as their masters, old is relative. Certainly we can all distinguish between a puppy West Highland White Terrier and an adult West Highland White Terrier—there are the obvious physical traits, such as size, appearance and facial expres-

sions, and personality traits. Puppies that are nasty are very rare. Puppies and young dogs like to play with children. Children's natural exuberance is a good match for the seemingly endless energy of young dogs. They like to run, jump, chase and retrieve. When dogs grow up and cease their interaction with children, they are often thought of as being too old to play with the kids.

On the other hand, if a West Highland White Terrier is only exposed to people over 60 years of age, its life will normally be less active and it will not seem to be getting old as its activity level slows down.

If people live to be 100 years old, dogs live to be 20 years old. Whilst this is a good rule of thumb, it is very inaccurate. When trying to compare dog years to human years, you cannot make a generalisation about all dogs. Terriers as a whole are long-lived dogs and your Westie will be no different. If your Westie lives to be eight years of age, you can be pretty certain that he will last

As your Westie gets older, his physical and mental abilities diminish. He deserves special attention from his owner during his golden years.

DID YOU KNOW?
The bottom line is simply that a dog is getting old when YOU think it is getting old because it slows down in its general activities, including walking, running, eating, jumping and retrieving. On the other hand, certain activities increase, like more sleeping, more barking and more repetition of habits like going to the door when you put your coat on without being called.

Opposite page: There is no fixed rule about how a Westie will act at any given age. Think about your human friends and how they change as time goes on.

until 12 years of age. I have friends who had four Westies that lived to be 14 to 16 years of age. Indeed, 16 years is a long time for a little white dog to live!

Dogs are generally considered mature within three years, but they can reproduce even earlier. So the first three years of a dog's life are like seven times that of comparable humans. That means a 3-year-old dog is like a 21-year-old human. As the curve of comparison shows, there is no hard and fast rule for comparing dog and human ages. The comparison is made even more difficult, for not all humans age at the same rate...and human females live longer than human males.

Sometimes older Westies become confused and less social and rarely come out to say hello. These are the times that your Westie needs additional reassurance.

WHAT TO LOOK FOR IN SENIORS

Most veterinary surgeons and behaviourists use the seventh year mark as the time to consider a dog a 'senior.' The term 'senior' does not imply that the dog is geriatric and has begun to fail in mind and body. Ageing is essentially a slowing process. Humans readily admit that they feel a difference in their activity level from age 20 to 30, and then from 30 to 40, etc. By treating the seven-year-old dog as a senior, owners are able to implement certain therapeutic and preventive medical strategies with the help of their veterinary surgeons. A senior-care programme should include at least two veterinary visits per year, screening sessions to determine the dog's health status, as well as nutritional counselling.

DID YOU KNOW?

Your senior dog may lose interest in eating, not because he's less hungry but because his senses of smell and taste have diminished. The old chow simply does not smell as good as it once did. Additionally, older dogs use less energy and thereby can sustain themselves on less food.

Veterinary surgeons determine the senior dog's health status through a blood smear for a complete blood count, serum chemistry profile with electrolytes, urinalysis, blood pressure check, electrocardiogram, ocular tonometry (pressure on the eyeball), and dental prophylaxis.

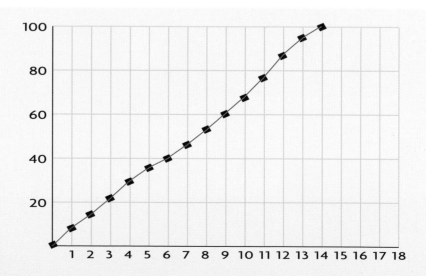

Such an extensive programme for senior dogs is well advised before owners start to see the obvious physical signs of ageing, such as slower and inhibited movement, greying, increased sleep/nap periods, and disinterest in play and other activity. This preventative programme promises a longer, healthier life for the ageing dog. Amongst the physical problems common in ageing dogs are the loss of sight and hearing, arthritis, kidney and liver failure, diabetes mellitus, heart disease, and Cushing's disease (a hormonal disease).

In addition to the physical manifestations discussed, there are some behavioural changes and problems related to ageing dogs. Dogs suffering from hearing or vision loss, dental discomfort or arthritis can become aggressive. Likewise the near-deaf and/or blind dog may be startled more easily and react in an unexpectedly aggressive manner. Seniors suffering from senility can become more impatient and irritable. Housesoiling accidents are associ-

ated with loss of mobility, kidney problems, loss of sphincter control as well as plaque accumulation, physiological brain changes, and reactions to medications. Older dogs, just like young puppies, suffer from separation anxiety, which can lead to excessive barking, whining, housesoiling, and destructive behaviour. Seniors may become fearful of everyday sounds, such

Senior dogs will not be able to perform the tasks and antics they enjoyed in their youth.

DID YOU KNOW?
The symptoms listed below are symptoms that gradually appear and become more noticeable. They are not life threatening; however, the symptoms below are to be taken very seriously and a discussion with your veterinary surgeon is warranted:

• Your dog cries and whimpers when it moves and stops running completely.

• Convulsions start or become more serious and frequent. The usual convulsion (spasm) is when the dog stiffens and starts to tremble being unable or unwilling to move. The seizure usually lasts for 5 to 30 minutes.

• Your dog drinks more water and urinates more frequently. Wetting and bowel accidents take place indoors without warning.

• Vomiting becomes more and more frequent.

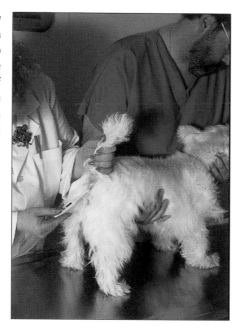

Your dog's body temperature is a good start to ascertaining the general health of your Westie. Learn how to do this yourself.

as vacuum cleaners, heaters, thunder, and passing traffic. Some dogs have difficulty sleeping, due to discomfort, the need for frequent potty visits, and the like. Owners should avoid spoiling the older dog with too many fatty treats. Obesity is a common problem in older dogs and subtracts years from their lifespan. Keep the senior dog as trim as possible since excessive weight puts additional stress on the body's vital organs. Some breeders recommend supplementing the diet with foods high in fibre and lower in calories. Adding fresh vegetables and marrow broth to the senior's diet makes a tasty, low-calorie, low-fat supplement. Vets also offer specialty diets for

senior dogs that are worth exploring.

Your dog, as he nears his twilight years, needs his owner's patience and good care more than ever. Never punish an older dog for an accident or abnormal behaviour. For all the years of love, protection and companionship that your dog has provided, he deserves special attention and courtesies. The older dog may need to relieve himself at 3 a.m. because he can no longer hold it for eight hours. Older dogs may not be able to remain crated for more than two or three hours. It may be time to give up a sofa or chair to your old friend. Although he may not seem as enthusiastic about your attention and petting, he does appreciate the considerations you offer as he gets older.

Your West Highland White Terrier does not understand why his world is slowing down. Owners must make the transition into the golden years as pleasant and rewarding as possible.

WHAT TO DO WHEN THE TIME COMES

You are never fully prepared to make a rational decision about putting your dog to sleep. It is very obvious that you love your West Highland White Terrier or you would not be reading this book. Putting a loved dog to sleep is extremely difficult. It is a decision that must be made with

CDS: COGNITIVE DYSFUNCTION SYNDROME
"Old Dog Syndrome"

There are many ways to evaluate old-dog syndrome. Veterinary surgeons have defined CDS (cognitive dysfunction syndrome) as the gradual deterioration of cognitive abilities. These are indicated by changes in the dog's behaviour. When a dog changes its routine response, and maladies have been eliminated as the cause of these behavioural changes, then CDS is the usual diagnosis.

More than half the dogs over 8 years old suffer some form of CDS. The older the dog, the more chance it has of suffering from CDS. In humans, doctors often dismiss the CDS behavioural changes as part of 'winding down.'

There are four major signs of CDS: frequent toilet accidents inside the home, sleeps much more or much less than normal, acts confused, and fails to respond to social stimuli.

SYMPTOMS OF CDS

FREQUENT TOILET ACCIDENTS
- *Urinates in the house.*
- *Defecates in the house.*
- *Doesn't signal that he wants to go out.*

SLEEP PATTERNS
- *Moves much more slowly.*
- *Sleeps more than normal during the day.*
- *Sleeps less during the night.*
- *Walks around listlessly and without a destination goal.*

CONFUSION
- *Goes outside and just stands there.*
- *Appears confused with a faraway look in his eyes.*
- *Hides more often.*
- *Doesn't recognise friends.*
- *Doesn't come when called.*

FAILS TO RESPOND TO SOCIAL STIMULI
- *Comes to people less frequently, whether called or not.*
- *Doesn't tolerate petting for more than a short time.*
- *Doesn't come to the door when you return home from work.*

your veterinary surgeon. You are usually forced to make the decision when one of the life-threatening symptoms listed above becomes serious enough for you to seek medical (veterinary) help.

If the prognosis of the malady indicates the end is near and your beloved pet will only suffer more and experience no enjoyment for the balance of its life, then euthanasia is the right choice.

WHAT IS EUTHANASIA?

Euthanasia derives from the Greek meaning *good death*. In other words, it means the planned, painless killing of a dog suffering

DID YOU KNOW?

The more open discussion you have about the whole stressful occurrence, the easier it will be for you when the time comes.

from a painful, incurable condition, or who is so aged that it cannot walk, see, eat or control its excretory functions.

Euthanasia is usually accomplished by injection with an overdose of an anaesthesia or barbiturate. Aside from the prick of the needle, the experience is painless.

Cemeteries for pets exists. Consult your veterinary surgeon to help you locate one.

Pet owners can choose to memorialise their deceased canine friends with special markers.

How About You?

The decision to euthanize your dog is never easy. The days during which the dog becomes ill and the end occurs can be unusually stressful for you. If this is your first experience with the death of a loved one, you may need the comfort dictated by your religious beliefs. If you are the head of the family and have children, you should have involved them in the decision of putting your West Highland White Terrier to sleep. Usually your dog can be maintained on drugs for a few days whilst it is kept in the clinic in order to give you ample time to make a decision. During this time, talking with members of the family or religious representatives, or even people who have lived through this same experience, can ease the burden of your inevitable decision. In any case, euthanasia is painful and stressful for the family of the dog. Unfortunately, it does not end there.

DID YOU KNOW?

Euthanasia must be done by a licensed veterinary surgeon. There also may be societies for the prevention of cruelty to animals in your area. They often offer this service upon a vet's recommendation.

THE FINAL RESTING PLACE

Dogs can have the same privileges as humans. They can be buried in a pet cemetery in a burial container (very expensive); buried in your garden in a place suitably marked with a stone, newly planted tree or bush; cremated with the ashes being given to you; or even stuffed and mounted by a taxidermist.

All of these options should be discussed frankly and openly with your veterinary surgeon. Do not be afraid to ask financial questions. Cremations are usually

Some pet cemeteries have inexpensive sites in which you can store your deceased pet's ashes.

mass burnings and the ashes you get may not be only the ashes of your beloved dog. If you want a private cremation, there are small crematoriums available to all veterinary clinics. Your vet can usually arrange for this but it may be a little more expensive.

GETTING ANOTHER DOG?

The grief of losing your beloved dog will be as lasting as the grief of losing a human friend or relative. You cannot go out and buy another grandfather, but you can go out and buy another West Highland White Terrier. In most cases, if your dog died of old age (if there is such a thing), it had slowed down considerably. Do you want a new West Highland White Terrier puppy to replace it? Or are you better off in finding a more mature West Highland White Terrier, say two to three years of age, which will usually be housetrained and will have an already developed personality. In this case, you can find out if you like each other after a few hours of being together.

The decision is, of course, your own. Do you want another West Highland White Terrier? Perhaps you want a smaller or larger dog? How much do you want to spend on a dog? Look in your local newspapers for advertisements (DOGS FOR SALE), or, better yet, consult your local society for the prevention of cruelty to animals to adopt a dog. It is harder to find puppies at an animal shelter, but there are often many adult dogs in need of new homes. You may be able to find another West Highland White Terrier, or you may choose another breed or a mixed-breed dog. Private breeders are the best source for high-quality puppies and dogs.

Whatever you decide, do it as quickly as possible. Most people usually buy the same breed.

West Highland White Terrier

As a West Highland White Terrier owner, you have selected your dog so that you and your loved ones can have a companion, a rodent patrolman, a friend and a four-legged family member. You invest time, money and effort to care for and train the family's new charge. Of course, this chosen canine behaves perfectly! Well, perfectly like a dog.

THINK LIKE A DOG

Dogs do not think like humans, nor do humans think like dogs, though we try. Unfortunately, a dog is incapable of figuring out how humans think, so the responsibility falls on the owner to adopt a proper canine mindset. Dogs cannot rationalise, and dogs exist in the present moment. Many dog owners make the mistake in training of thinking that they can reprimand their dog for something he did a while ago. Basically, you cannot even reprimand a dog for something he did 20 seconds ago! Either catch him in the act or forget it! It is a waste of your and your dog's time—in his mind, you are reprimanding him for whatever he is doing at that moment.

The following behavioural problems represent some which owners most commonly encounter. Every dog is unique and every situation is unique. No author could purport to solve your West Highland White Terrier's problem simply by reading a script. Here we outline some basic 'dogspeak' so that owners' chances of solving behavioural problems are increased. Discuss bad habits with your veterinary surgeon and he/she can recommend a behavioural specialist to consult in appropriate cases. Since behavioural abnormalities are the leading reason owners abandon their pets, we hope that you will make a valiant effort to solve your West Highland White Terrier's problem. Patience and

DID YOU KNOW?
Dogs and humans may be the only animals that smile. Dogs imitate the smile on their owner's face when he greets a friend. The dog only smiles at its human friends. It never smiles at another dog or cat. Usually it rolls up its lips and shows its teeth in a clenched mouth while it rolls over onto its back begging for a soft scratch.

DID YOU KNOW?

Punishment is rarely necessary for a misbehaving dog. Dogs that are habitually bad probably had a poor education and they do not know what is expected of them. They need training. Disciplinary behaviour on your part usually does more harm than good.

understanding are virtues that dwell in every pet-loving household.

AGGRESSION

This is a problem that concerns some owners of West Highland White Terriers. Aggression can be a very big problem in dogs, especially in terriers that do not readily accept other canines. Aggression, when not controlled, always becomes dangerous. An aggressive dog, no matter the size, may lunge at, bite or even attack a person or another dog. Aggressive behaviour is not to be tolerated. It is painful for a family to watch their dog become unpredictable in his behaviour to the point where they are afraid of him. Whilst not all aggressive behaviour is dangerous, growling, baring teeth, etc., can be frightening: It is important to ascertain why the dog is acting in

this manner. Aggression is a display of dominance, and the dog should not have the dominant role in its pack, which is, in this case, your family.

It is important not to challenge an aggressive dog as this could provoke an attack. Observe your West Highland White Terrier's body language. Does he make direct eye contact and stare? Does he try to make himself as large as possible: ears pricked, chest out, tail erect? Height and size signify authority in a dog pack—being taller or 'above' another dog literally means that he is 'above' in the social status. These body signals tell you that your West Highland White Terrier thinks he is

DID YOU KNOW?

Dog aggression is a serious problem. NEVER give an aggressive dog to someone else. The dog will usually be more aggressive in a new situation where his leadership is unchallenged and unquestioned (in his mind).

in charge, a problem that needs to be addressed. An aggressive dog is unpredictable: you never know when he is going to strike and what he is going to do. You cannot understand why a dog that is playful and loving one minute is growling and snapping the next.

Few things are as rewarding as a family of Westies, beautifully preserved in this portrait.

Well-socialised puppies, which have proper introductions to other dogs, will grow up to be more accepting of other canines.

The best solution is to consult a behavioural specialist, one who has experience with the West Highland White Terrier if possible. Together, perhaps you can pinpoint the cause of your dog's aggression and do something about it. An aggressive dog cannot be trusted, and a dog that cannot be trusted is not safe to have as a family pet. If the pet Westie becomes untrustworthy, he cannot be kept in the home with the family. The family must get rid of the dog. In the worst case, the dog must be euthanized.

DID YOU KNOW?

DANGER! If you and your on-lead dog are approached by a larger, running dog that is not restrained, walk away from the dog as quickly as possible. Don't allow your dog to make eye contact with the other dog. You should not make eye contact either. In dog terms, eye contact indicates a challenge.

AGGRESSION TOWARD OTHER DOGS

In general, a dog's aggressive behaviour toward another dog stems from not enough exposure to other dogs at an early age. In West Highland White Terriers, early socialisation with other dogs is absolutely essential since most terriers are feisty around other dogs. If other dogs make your West Highland White Terrier nervous and agitated, he will lash out as a defensive mechanism. A dog who has not received sufficient exposure to other canines tends to believe that he is the only dog on

DID YOU KNOW?

If you are approached by an aggressive, growling dog, do not run away. Simply stand still and avoid eye contact. If you have something in your hand (like a handbag), throw it sideways away from your body to distract the dog from making a frontal attack.

the planet. The animal becomes so dominant that he does not even show signs that he is fearful or threatened. Without growling or any other physical signal as a warning, he will lunge at and bite the other dog. A way to correct this is to let your West Highland White Terrier approach another dog when walking on lead. Watch very

closely and at the very first sign of aggression, correct your West Highland White Terrier and pull him away. Scold him for any sign of discomfort, and then praise him when he ignores or tolerates the other dog. Keep this up until he stops the aggressive behaviour, learns to ignore the other dog or accepts other dogs. Praise him lavishly for his correct behaviour.

Dominant Aggression

A social hierarchy is firmly established in a wild dog pack. The dog wants to dominate those under him and please those above him. Dogs know that there must be a leader. If you are not the obvious choice for emperor, the dog will assume the throne! These conflicting innate desires are what a dog owner is up against when he sets about training a dog. In training a dog to obey commands, the owner is reinforcing that he is the top dog in the 'pack' and that the dog

DID YOU KNOW?
Fear in a grown dog is often the result of improper or incomplete socialisation as a pup, or it can be the result of a traumatic experience he suffered when young. Keep in mind that the term 'traumatic' is relative—something that you would not think twice about can leave a lasting negative impression on a puppy. If the dog experiences a similar experience later in life, he may try to fight back to protect himself. Again, this behaviour is very unpredictable, especially if you do not know what is triggering his fear.

DID YOU KNOW?
Your dog inherited the pack-leader mentality. He only knows about pecking order. He instinctively wants to be top dog but you have to convince him that you are boss. There is no such thing as living in a democracy with your dog; you must be the one in control.

should, and should want to, serve his superior. Thus, the owner is suppressing the dog's urge to dominate by modifying his behaviour and making him obedient.

An important part of training is taking every opportunity to reinforce that you are the leader. The simple action of making your West Highland White Terrier sit to wait for his food says that you control when he eats and that he is dependent on you for food. Although it may be difficult, do not give in to your dog's wishes every time he whines at you or looks at you with his pleading eyes. It is a constant effort to show the dog that his place in the pack is at the bottom. This is not meant to sound cruel or inhumane. You love your Westie and you should treat him with care and affection. You (hopefully) did not get a dog just so you could boss around another creature. Dog training is not about being cruel or feeling important, it is about moulding the dog's behaviour into what is acceptable

DID YOU KNOW?

Never allow your puppy to growl at you or bare his tiny teeth. Such behaviour is dominant and aggressive. If not corrected, the dog will repeat the behaviour, which will become more threatening as he grows larger and will eventually lead to biting.

DID YOU KNOW?

When a dog bites there is always a good reason for it doing so. Many dogs are trained to protect a person, an area or an object. When that person, area or object is violated, the dog will attack. A dog attacks with its mouth. It has no other means of attack. It never uses teeth for defense. It merely runs away or lays down on the ground when it is in an indefensible situation. Fighting dogs (and there are many breeds which fight) are taught to fight, but they also have a natural instinct to fight. This instinct is normally reserved for other dogs, though unfortunate accidents occur when a baby crawls towards a fighting dog and the dog mistakes the crawling child as a potential attacker.

If a dog is a biter for no reason, if it bites the hand that feeds it or if it snaps at members of your family, see your veterinary surgeon or behaviourist immediately to learn how to modify the dog's behaviour.

and teaching him to live by your rules. In theory, it is quite simple: catch him in appropriate behaviour and reward him for it. Add a dog into the equation and it becomes a bit more trying, but as a rule of thumb, positive reinforcement is what works best.

With a dominant dog, punishment and negative reinforcement can have the opposite effect of what you are after. It can make a dog fearful and/or act out aggressively if he feels he is being challenged. Remember, a dominant dog perceives himself at the top of the social heap and will fight to defend his perceived status. The best way to prevent that is never to give him reason to think that he is in control in the first place. If you are having trouble training your West Highland White Terrier and it seems as if he is constantly challenging your authority, seek the help of an obedience trainer or behavioural specialist. A profes-

DID YOU KNOW?

Never scream, shout, jump or run about if you want your dog to stay calm. You set the example for your dog's behaviour in most circumstances. Learn from your dog's reaction to your behaviour and act accordingly.

sional will work with both you and your dog to teach you effective techniques to use at home. Beware of trainers who rely on excessively harsh methods; scolding is necessary now and then, but the focus in your training should always be on positive reinforcement.

If you can isolate what brings out the fear reaction, you can help the dog get over it. Supervise your West Highland White Terrier's interactions with people and other dogs, and praise the dog when it goes well. If he starts to act aggressively in a situation, correct him and remove him from the situation. Do not let people approach the dog and start petting him without your express permission. That way, you can have the dog sit to accept petting, and praise him when he behaves properly. You are focusing on praise and on modifying his behaviour by rewarding him when he acts appropriately. By being gentle and by supervising his

interactions, you are showing him that there is no need to be afraid or defensive.

SEXUAL BEHAVIOUR

Dogs exhibit certain sexual behaviours that may have influenced your choice of male or female when you first purchased your West Highland White Terrier. Spaying/neutering will eliminate these behaviours, but if you are purchasing a dog that you wish to breed, you should be aware of what you will have to deal with throughout the dog's life.

Female dogs usually have two oestruses per year with each season lasting about three weeks. These are the only times in which a

DID YOU KNOW?

We all love our dogs and our dogs love us. They show their love and affection by licking us. This is not a very sanitary practice as dogs lick and sniff in some unsavory places. Kissing your dog on the mouth is strictly forbidden, as parasites can be transmitted in this manner.

female dog will mate, and she usually will not allow this until the second week of the cycle. If a bitch is not bred during the heat cycle, it is not uncommon for her to experience a false pregnancy, in which her mammary glands swell and she exhibits maternal tendencies toward toys or other objects.

Owners must further recognise that mounting is not merely a sexual expression but also one of dominance. Be consistent and persistent and you will find that you can 'move mounters.'

DID YOU KNOW?
Males, whether castrated or not, will mount almost anything: a pillow, your leg or, much to your horror, even your neighbour's leg. As with other types of inappropriate behaviour, the dog must be corrected while in the act, which for once is not difficult. Often he will not let go! While a puppy is experimenting with his very first urges, his owners feel he needs to 'sow his oats' and allow the pup to mount. As the pup grows into a full-size dog, with full-size urges, it becomes a nuisance and an embarrassment. Males always appear as if they are trying to 'save the race,' more determined and stronger than imaginable. While altering the dog at an appropriate age will limit the dog's desire, it usually does not remove it entirely.

DID YOU KNOW?
Dogs get to know each other by sniffing each other's backsides. It seems that each dog has a telltale odor probably created by the anal glands. It also distinguishes sex and signals when a female will be receptive to a male's attention. Some dog's snap at the other dog's intrusion of their private parts.

CHEWING
The national canine pastime is chewing! Every dog loves to sink his 'canines' into a tasty bone, but sometimes that bone is attached to his owner's hand! Dogs need to chew, to massage their gums, to make their new teeth feel better and to exercise their jaws. This is a natural behaviour deeply imbedded in all things canine. Our role as owners is not to stop chewing, but to redirect it to positive, chew-worthy objects. Be an informed owner and purchase proper chew toys like strong nylon bones made for active dogs like your Westie. Be sure that the devices are safe and durable, since your dog's safety is at risk. Again, the owner is responsible for ensuring a dog-proof environment. The best answer is prevention: that is, put your shoes, handbags and other tasty objects in their proper places (out of the reach

of the growing canine mouth). Direct puppies to their toys whenever you see them tasting the furniture legs or your pant leg. Make a loud noise to attract the

pup's attention and immediately escort him to his chew toy and engage him with the toy for at least four minutes, praising and encouraging him all the while.

Some trainers recommend deterrents, such as hot pepper or another bitter spice or a product designed for this purpose, to discourage the dog from chewing unwanted objects. This is sometimes reliable, though not as often as the manufacturers of such products claim. Test out the product with your own dog before investing in a case of it.

JUMPING UP

Jumping up is a dog's friendly way of saying hello! Some dog owners do not mind when their dog jumps up, which is fine for them. The problem arises when guests come to the house and the dog greets them in the same manner—whether they like it or not! However friendly the greeting may be, chances are your visitors will not appreciate being knocked over by your boister-

Chewing is as natural to a dog as breathing and barking! These puppies are attacking some new chew toys that are made safe for dogs.

Even a well-trained Westie may jump up on you (with his dirty feet) if he is happy to see you.

149

ous West Highland White Terrier. The dog will not be able to distinguish upon whom he can jump and whom he cannot. Therefore, it is probably best to discourage this behaviour entirely.

Pick a command such as 'Off.' (avoid using 'Down' since you will use that for the dog to lie down) and tell him 'Off' when he jumps up. Place him on the ground on all fours and have him sit, praising him the whole time. Always lavish him with praise and petting when he is in the sit position. That way you are still giving him a warm affectionate greeting, because you are as excited to see him as he is to see you!

DIGGING

Digging, which is seen as a destructive behaviour to humans, is actually quite a natural behaviour in dogs, especially terriers. A Westie's desire to dig can be irrepressible and most frustrating to his owners, who have to bathe him every time he hits the mud! When digging occurs in your garden, it is actually a normal behaviour redirected into something the dog can do in his everyday life. In the wild, a dog would be actively seeking food, making his own shelter, etc. He would be using his paws in a purposeful manner for his survival. Since you provide him with food and shelter, he has no need to use his paws for these purposes, and so the energy that he would be using

manifests itself in the form of little holes all over your garden and flower beds.

Perhaps your dog is digging as a reaction to boredom—it is somewhat similar to someone eating a whole bag of crisps in front of the TV—because they are there and there is not anything better to do! Basically, the answer is to provide the dog with adequate play and exercise so that his mind and paws are occupied, and so that he feels as if he is doing something useful.

Of course, digging is easiest to control if it is stopped as soon as possible, but it is often hard to catch a dog in the act, especially if he is alone in the garden during the day. If your dog is a compulsive digger and is not easily distracted by other activities, you can designate an area on your property where it is okay for him to dig. If you catch him digging in an off-limits area of the garden, immedi-

DID YOU KNOW?

If your dog barks or growls at strangers, or growls at anyone coming near his food while he is eating, playing with a toy or taking a rest in his favourite spot, he needs proper professional training because sooner or later this behaviour can result in someone being bitten.

Training your photogenic Westie to respect the daffodils is quite a difficult task. It's best to keep your terrier away from your flowerbeds!

he excited, happy, frightened or angry? Whatever it is that the dog is trying to say, he should not be punished for barking. Only when the barking becomes excessive, and when the excessive barking becomes a bad habit, does the behaviour need to be modified. Terriers tend to be a wee bit barky, though Westies tend to bark more purposefully than the other terriers. If an intruder came into your home in the middle of the night and your West Highland White Terrier

ately bring him to the approved area and praise him for digging there. Keep a close eye on him so that you can catch him in the act—that is the only way to make him understand what is permitted and what is not. If you bring him to a hole he dug an hour ago and tell him 'No,' he will understand that you are not fond of holes, or dirt, or flowers. If you catch him whilst he is stifle-deep in your tulips, that is when he will get your message.

BARKING

Dogs cannot talk—oh, what they would say if they could! Instead, barking is a dog's way of 'talking.' It can be somewhat frustrating because it is not always easy to tell what a dog means by his bark—is barked a warning, you would be pleased. You would probably deem your dog a hero, a wonderful guardian and protector of the home. Barking at every outdoor noise, however, may not be welcome. For instance, if a friend drops by unexpectedly and rings the doorbell and is greeted with a sudden sharp bark, you would probably be annoyed at the dog. But in reality, this is the very same behaviour that pleased you earlier. The dog does not know any better…unless he sees who is at the door and it is someone he knows, he will bark as a means of vocalising that his (and your) territory is being threatened. Whilst your friend is not posing a threat, it is all the same to the dog. Barking is his means of letting you know that there is an intrusion, whether friend or foe, on your property. This type of barking is instinctive and should not be discouraged.

Excessive habitual barking, however, is a problem that should be corrected early on. As your Westie grows up, you will be able to tell when his barking is purposeful and when it is for no reason. You will become able to distinguish your dog's different barks and their meanings. For example, the bark when someone comes to the door will be different from the bark when he is excited to see you. It is similar to a person's tone of voice, except that the dog has to rely totally on tone of voice because he

does not have the benefit of using words. An incessant barker will be evident at an early age.

There are some things that encourage a dog to bark. For example, if your dog barks non-stop for a few minutes and you give him a treat to quiet him, he believes that you are rewarding him for barking. He will associate barking with getting a treat, and will keep doing it until he is rewarded.

FOOD STEALING
Is your dog devising ways of stealing food from your cupboard? If so, you must answer the following questions: Is your West Highland White Terrier hungry, or is he 'constantly famished' like every other chow hound? Why is there food on the counter top? Face it, some dogs are more food-motivated than others. Some dogs are totally obsessed by a slab of brisket and can only think of their next meal. Food stealing is terrific fun and always yields a great reward—FOOD, glorious food.

The owner's goal, therefore, is to make the 'reward' less rewarding, even startling! Plant a shaker can (an empty pop can with coins inside) on the counter so that it catches your pooch offguard. There are other devices available that will surprise the dog when he is looking for a mid-afternoon snack. Such remote-control devices, though not the first choice of some trainers, allow the correction to come from

the object instead of the owner. These devices are also useful to keep the snacking hound from napping on furniture that is forbidden.

BEGGING

Just like food stealing, begging is a favourite pastime of hungry puppies! It yields that same lovely reward—FOOD! Dogs quickly learn that their owners keep the 'good food' for themselves, and that we humans do not dine on kibble alone. Begging is a conditioned response related to a specific stimulus, time and place. The sounds of the kitchen, cans and bottles opening, crinkling bags, the smell of food in preparation, etc., will excite the chow hound and soon the paws are in the air!

Here is the solution to stopping this behaviour: Never give in to a beggar! You are rewarding the dog for sitting pretty, jumping up, whining and rubbing his nose into you by giving him that glorious reward—food. By ignoring the dog, you will (eventually) force the

behaviour into extinction. Note that the behaviour likely gets worse before it disappears, so be sure there are not any 'softies' in the family who will give in to little 'Oliver' every time he whimpers, 'More, please.'

SEPARATION ANXIETY

Your West Highland White Terrier may howl, whine or otherwise vocalise his displeasure at your leaving the house and his being left alone. This is a normal case of separation anxiety, and there are things that can be done to eliminate this problem. Your dog needs to learn that he will be fine on his own for a while and that he will not wither away if he is not attended to every minute of the day. In fact, constant attention can lead to separation anxiety in the first place. If you are endlessly coddling and cooing over your dog, he will come

Stealing and begging are unattractive habits in any dog. Your Westie must understand the house rules from early puppyhood, or else your adult might take over your home (and office).

DID YOU KNOW?
Dogs left alone for varying lengths of time may often react wildly when you return. Sometimes they run, jump, bite, chew, tear things apart, wet themselves, gobble their food or behave in a very undisciplined manner. Allow them to calm down before greeting them or they will consider your attention as a reward for their antics.

to expect this from you all of the time and it will be more traumatic for him when you are not there. Obviously, you enjoy spending time with your dog, and he thrives on your love and attention. However, it should not become a dependent relationship where he is heartbroken without you.

One thing you can do to minimise separation anxiety is to make your entrances and exits as low-key as possible. Do not give your dog a long drawn-out goodbye, and do not lavish him with hugs and kisses when you return. This is giving in to the attention that he craves, and it will only make him miss it more when you are away. Another thing you can try is to give your dog a treat when you leave; this will not only

Separation anxiety is one of a Westie's worst fears. Whenever you must leave your Westie alone, secure him in his dog-proof area in the home rather than letting him roam free.

keep him occupied and keep his mind off the fact that you just left, but it will also help him associate your leaving with a pleasant experience.

You may have to accustom your

dog to being left alone in intervals, much like when you introduced your pup to his crate. Of course, when your dog starts whimpering as you approach the door, your first instinct will be to run to him and comfort him, but do not do it! Really—eventually he will adjust and be just fine if you take it in small steps. His anxiety stems from being placed in an unfamiliar situation; by familiarising him with being alone he will learn that he is okay. That is not to say you should purposely leave your dog home alone, but the dog needs to know that whilst he can depend on you for his care, you do not have to be by his side 24 hours a day.

When the dog is alone in the house, he should be confined to his crate or a designated dog-proof area of the house. This should be the area in which he sleeps and already feels comfortable so he will feel more at ease when he is alone. This

DID YOU KNOW?

There are two drugs specifically designed to treat mental problems in dogs. About 7 million dogs each year are destroyed because owners can no longer tolerate their dogs' behaviour, according to Nicholas Dodman, a specialist in animal behaviour at Tufts University in Massachusetts.

The first drug, Clomicalm, is prescribed for dogs suffering from 'separation anxiety,' which is said to cause them to react when left alone by barking, chewing their owners' belongings, drooling copiously, or defecating or urinating inside the home.

The second drug, Anipryl, is recommended for canine cognitive dysfunction or 'old dog syndrome,' a mental deterioration that comes with age. Such dogs often seem to forget that they were housebroken, where their food bowls are, and they may even fail to recognise their owners.

A tremendous human-animal-bonding relationship is established with all dogs, particularly senior dogs. This precious relationship deteriorates when the dog does not recognise his master. The drug can restore the bond and make senior dogs feel more like their old selves.

is just one of the many examples in which a crate is an invaluable tool for you and your dog, and another reinforcement of why your dog should view his crate as a 'happy' place, a place of his own.

COPROPHAGIA

Faeces eating is, to most humans, one of the most disgusting behaviours that their dog could engage in, yet to the dog it is perfectly normal. It is hard for us to understand why a dog would want to eat its own faeces. He could be seeking certain nutrients that are missing from his diet; he could be just plain hungry; or he could be attracted by the pleasing (to a dog) scent. Whilst coprophagia most often refers to the dog eating his own faeces, a dog may eat that of another animal as well if he comes across it. Vets have found that diets with a low digestibility, containing relatively low levels of fibre and high levels of starch, increase coprophagia. Therefore, high-fibre diets may, decrease the likelihood of dogs eating faeces. Both the consistency of the stool (how firm it feels in the dog's mouth) and the presence of undigested nutrients increase the likelihood. Dogs often find the stool of cats and horses more palatable than that of other dogs. Once the dog develops diarrhoea from faeces eating, it will likely quit this distasteful habit, since dogs tend to prefer eating harder faeces.

INDEX

*Page numbers in **boldface** indicate illustrations.*

My West Highland White Terrier

PUT YOUR PUPPY'S FIRST PICTURE HERE

Dog's Name _____

Date _____ Photographer _____